SPECTRUM

Math

Grade 5

School Specialty.
Publishing

Columbus, Ohio

Send all inquiries to:
School Specialty Publishing
8720 Orion Place
Columbus, OH 43240-2111

ISBN 0-7696-3705-1

6 7 8 9 10 HPS 11 10 09

Table of Contents Grade 5

Table of Contents, continued

Check What You Know

Adding and Subtracting through 6 Digits

Add or subtract.

	a	b	c	d	e
1.	27 +36	62 +45	18 +66	34 +68	83 +57
2.	391 +542	738 +467	438 +364	927 +576	1583 +9769
3.	1264 +4256	5372 +2418	28261 + 9472	19506 +63475	32471 +84266
4.	323 406 +721	7823 147 + 394	3642 5194 +1476	24742 4516 + 6327	52162 27413 +82764
5.	68 −32	76 −51	54 −26	83 −47	72 −55
6.	236 − 47	617 − 58	529 − 99	332 −164	763 −345
7.	5726 − 384	8639 − 884	2176 − 399	6318 − 420	9631 −4378
8.	17632 − 3461	27563 − 4828	83612 − 7384	29446 − 2739	63104 −21847

Check What You Know

CHAPTER 1 PRETEST

Adding and Subtracting through 6 Digits

Circle Add or Subtract. Solve each problem.

9. There are 17 campers in Lucy's group and 22 campers in Raku's group. How many campers are in the two groups?

Add   Subtract

There are _____ campers in the two groups.

9.

10. There are 23 students in Ms. Horan's class, 36 students in Mrs. Robinson's class, and 27 students in Mr. Campos's class. How many students are in the three classes?

Add   Subtract

There are _____ students in the three classes.

10.

11. Manuel has 19 quarters, 36 dimes, 58 nickels, and 143 pennies. How many coins does Manuel have?

Add   Subtract

Manuel has _____ coins.

11.

12. The Seahawks lost to the Rovers in the basketball game. The Seahawks scored 69 points and the Rovers scored 98 points. How many more points did the Rovers score than the Seahawks?

Add   Subtract

The Rovers scored _____ more points.

12.

13. Ann Marie must sell 5,624 cookies to win a trip. She has sold 875 cookies. How many more cookies does Ann Marie need to sell?

Add   Subtract

Ann Marie needs to sell _____ more cookies.

13.

Lesson 1.1   Adding and Subtracting 2 and 3 Digits

Add the ones.
$7 + 5 = 12$
Rename 12 as
1 ten and 2 ones.

Add the tens.

Rename 322 as
3 hundreds, 1 ten,
and 12 ones.
Subtract the ones.

Rename 3 hundreds
and 1 ten as 2
hundreds and
11 tens.
Subtract the tens.

addend
$\begin{array}{r} 67 \\ +45 \\ \hline \end{array}$
$\begin{array}{r} 7 \\ +\ 5 \\ \hline ①2 \end{array}$
$\begin{array}{r} 67 \\ +45 \\ \hline 2 \end{array}$
$\begin{array}{r} 1 \\ 67 \\ +45 \\ \hline 112 \end{array}$
sum

minuend
$\begin{array}{r} 322 \\ -\ 56 \\ \hline \end{array}$
$\begin{array}{r} {}^{1\ 12} \\ 3\cancel{2}\cancel{2} \\ -\ 56 \\ \hline 6 \end{array}$
subtrahend

$\begin{array}{r} {}^{2\ 11\ 12} \\ \cancel{3}\cancel{2}\cancel{2} \\ -\ 56 \\ \hline 266 \end{array}$
difference

Add or subtract.

	a	b	c	d	e	f
1.	$\begin{array}{r} 12 \\ +34 \\ \hline \end{array}$	$\begin{array}{r} 49 \\ +22 \\ \hline \end{array}$	$\begin{array}{r} 37 \\ +18 \\ \hline \end{array}$	$\begin{array}{r} 50 \\ +76 \\ \hline \end{array}$	$\begin{array}{r} 64 \\ +46 \\ \hline \end{array}$	$\begin{array}{r} 98 \\ +36 \\ \hline \end{array}$
2.	$\begin{array}{r} 56 \\ +73 \\ \hline \end{array}$	$\begin{array}{r} 76 \\ +33 \\ \hline \end{array}$	$\begin{array}{r} 52 \\ +18 \\ \hline \end{array}$	$\begin{array}{r} 29 \\ +67 \\ \hline \end{array}$	$\begin{array}{r} 41 \\ +89 \\ \hline \end{array}$	$\begin{array}{r} 98 \\ +25 \\ \hline \end{array}$
3.	$\begin{array}{r} 22 \\ +77 \\ \hline \end{array}$	$\begin{array}{r} 35 \\ +14 \\ \hline \end{array}$	$\begin{array}{r} 27 \\ +61 \\ \hline \end{array}$	$\begin{array}{r} 43 \\ +32 \\ \hline \end{array}$	$\begin{array}{r} 11 \\ +93 \\ \hline \end{array}$	$\begin{array}{r} 41 \\ +16 \\ \hline \end{array}$
4.	$\begin{array}{r} 65 \\ -34 \\ \hline \end{array}$	$\begin{array}{r} 77 \\ -14 \\ \hline \end{array}$	$\begin{array}{r} 48 \\ -23 \\ \hline \end{array}$	$\begin{array}{r} 99 \\ -58 \\ \hline \end{array}$	$\begin{array}{r} 62 \\ -36 \\ \hline \end{array}$	$\begin{array}{r} 84 \\ -25 \\ \hline \end{array}$
5.	$\begin{array}{r} 43 \\ -28 \\ \hline \end{array}$	$\begin{array}{r} 57 \\ -39 \\ \hline \end{array}$	$\begin{array}{r} 61 \\ -15 \\ \hline \end{array}$	$\begin{array}{r} 52 \\ -24 \\ \hline \end{array}$	$\begin{array}{r} 83 \\ -26 \\ \hline \end{array}$	$\begin{array}{r} 163 \\ -\ 67 \\ \hline \end{array}$
6.	$\begin{array}{r} 95 \\ -57 \\ \hline \end{array}$	$\begin{array}{r} 143 \\ -\ 89 \\ \hline \end{array}$	$\begin{array}{r} 213 \\ -\ 25 \\ \hline \end{array}$	$\begin{array}{r} 162 \\ -\ 88 \\ \hline \end{array}$	$\begin{array}{r} 474 \\ -\ 97 \\ \hline \end{array}$	$\begin{array}{r} 721 \\ -\ 98 \\ \hline \end{array}$

Lesson 1.2 Adding and Subtracting 3 and 4 Digits

Add from right to left.

$$
\begin{array}{r}
{}^{1}\ \ \\
3\,7\,6 \\
+\,9\,4\,8 \\
\hline
4
\end{array}
\qquad
\begin{array}{r}
{}^{1\,1}\ \\
3\,7\,6 \\
+\,9\,4\,8 \\
\hline
2\,4
\end{array}
\qquad
\begin{array}{r}
{}^{1\,1}\ \\
3\,7\,6 \\
+\ \ 9\,4\,8 \\
\hline
1\,3\,2\,4
\end{array}
$$

addend ← 376   376   376
+948 +948 + 948

sum

Subtract from right to left.

minuend → 8 4 7 2   8 4 7 2   8 4 7 2
− 685   − 685   − 685
7   87   7787

subtrahend   difference

Add or subtract.

	a	b	c	d	e	f
1.	234 +763	479 +210	651 +142	826 +152	350 +519	115 +453
2.	367 +526	175 +226	418 +567	363 +194	229 +685	891 +609
3.	749 +813	584 +558	924 +457	637 +485	948 +893	716 +987
4.	563 −429	756 −598	634 −126	957 −278	572 −238	827 −435
5.	790 −348	405 −178	682 −297	4692 − 357	5360 − 824	3179 − 690
6.	1579 − 594	6943 − 758	7631 − 655	3722 − 888	4962 − 779	2486 − 938
7.	3281 − 968	5826 − 979	8493 − 629	6924 − 937	8562 − 276	9392 − 763

Lesson 1.3 Adding and Subtracting 4 through 6 Digits

Add from right to left.

	¹	¹ ¹	¹ ¹ ¹	¹ ¹ ¹ ¹
addend →	319365	319365	319365	319365
addend →	+ 23879	+ 23879	+ 23879	+ 23879
Sum →	4	44	244	343244

Subtract from right to left.

minuend →	746¹³	5 0¹³ 7461̸3̸	3 5̸ 0¹³ 7̸461̸3̸	6 2̸ 5̸ 0¹³ 7̸461̸3̸
subtrahend →	– 9854	– 9854	– 9854	– 9854
difference →	9	59	759	64759

Add or subtract.

	a	b	c	d	e
1.	4726 +3261	6257 +4238	7192 +4567	12506 +37324	92184 +46837
2.	3642 −1340	9350 −1227	8058 −7739	76429 −32847	26413 −17387
3.	28944 +26375	59617 +74623	86082 +28379	15726 +29935	374926 + 18347
4.	47962 −19628	39741 −21964	58342 −26797	296378 − 37492	739761 − 43785
5.	636214 + 39488	929917 + 51485	236479 + 83515	259678 +146938	822419 +637597
6.	843715 − 67348	629763 −317687	374014 −278306	791632 −345956	945196 −176347

Lesson 1.4 Problem Solving

SHOW YOUR WORK

Circle Add or Subtract. Solve each problem.

1. Marcus scored 23 points in his basketball game on Friday and 19 points in his basketball game on Saturday. How many points did Marcus score in two games? Add Subtract Marcus scored _____ points in two games.	**1.**
2. Alisa, Jamie, and Christina are planning a movie night. The first movie is 103 minutes long and the second movie is 124 minutes long. How long will it take to watch both movies? Add Subtract It will take _____ minutes to watch both movies.	**2.**
3. Ms. Oakwood needs 8,391 strawberries to bake her pies. She has picked 374 strawberries. How many more strawberries does Ms. Oakwood need? Add Subtract Ms. Oakwood must pick _____ more strawberries.	**3.**
4. The Yuens are driving across the country. The trip is 3,281 miles. They have driven 2,596 miles. How many more miles do they have left to drive? Add Subtract There are _____ miles left to drive.	**4.**
5. Alicia and Peter are reading the same book. Alicia has read 297 pages and Peter has read 431 pages. How many more pages has Peter read than Alicia? Add Subtract Peter has read _____ more pages than Alicia.	**5.**

Lesson 1.5 Adding 3 or More Numbers
(3 through 6 digits)

Add the ones.	Add the tens.	Add the hundreds.	Add the thousands.	Add the ten thousands.
²	¹ ²	² ¹ ²	² ² ¹ ²	¹ ² ² ¹ ²
36718	36718	36718	36718	36718
74916	74916	74916	74916	74916
13455	13455	13455	13455	13455
+ 48286	+ 48286	+ 48286	+ 48286	+ 48286
5	75	375	3375	173375

Add.

	a	b	c	d	e
1.	562	433	637	479	7763
	124	781	945	834	246
	+278	+729	+862	+326	+ 197
2.	372	2782	12633	37563	240329
	497	3521	5067	497	17633
	634	617	2451	21474	46395
	+403	+ 235	+ 263	+ 8631	+ 24771
3.	426	2394	59723	23847	769431
	391	626	4571	51726	47253
	673	3144	1436	8623	32296
	481	990	3814	3439	1473
	+182	+ 212	+ 743	+ 612	+ 2914
4.	795	3489	65913	21963	425693
	818	1065	4761	15172	219742
	213	7623	9374	56499	163994
	469	594	2618	7155	37443
	554	369	342	1894	11217
	+824	+ 182	+ 534	+ 3765	+ 67347

Lesson 1.6 Addition and Subtraction Practice

Add or subtract.

	a	b	c	d	e
1.	89 +97	54 +86	946 +378	219 +635	5623 + 739
2.	2397 +6947	8046 +3556	42198 + 7341	16749 +37582	246297 +365918
3.	613 295 +672	4763 2942 +1375	25791 4652 + 9372	7613 44964 +36247	19624 823579 + 54218
4.	76235 14378 +15624	232631 348923 +217598	482 376 927 +216	2481 3623 737 +6914	68372 5719 43622 +18946
5.	43 −17	96 −57	63 −29	74 −58	369 − 86
6.	175 − 68	736 − 98	871 −386	5362 − 437	9213 −4086
7.	3554 −1837	8216 −3435	4195 −3817	76516 − 2839	41935 − 6458
8.	68142 −26324	94909 −57342	716426 − 83198	183650 − 94667	852136 −347028

Lesson 1.7   Estimating Sums and Differences

Estimate numbers. Add from right to left.

$$
\begin{array}{r}
64281 \longrightarrow 60000 \\
+58644 \longrightarrow +\ 60000 \\
\hline
120000
\end{array}
$$

Estimate numbers. Subtract from right to left.

$$
\begin{array}{r}
83629 \longrightarrow 84000 \\
-\ 5274 \longrightarrow -\ 5000 \\
\hline
79000
\end{array}
$$

Round each number to the highest place value the numbers have in common.

If the number in the next highest place is greater than 5, round up.

Estimate numbers. Add or subtract.

	a	b	c	d
1.	$\begin{array}{r} 2614 \\ +3196 \\ \hline \end{array}$	$\begin{array}{r} 4617 \\ +3724 \\ \hline \end{array}$	$\begin{array}{r} 2453 \\ +3257 \\ \hline \end{array}$	$\begin{array}{r} 12450 \\ +73876 \\ \hline \end{array}$
2.	$\begin{array}{r} 8376 \\ -4917 \\ \hline \end{array}$	$\begin{array}{r} 36451 \\ -\ 2732 \\ \hline \end{array}$	$\begin{array}{r} 64730 \\ -18634 \\ \hline \end{array}$	$\begin{array}{r} 86536 \\ -27423 \\ \hline \end{array}$
3.	$\begin{array}{r} 13645 \\ +62773 \\ \hline \end{array}$	$\begin{array}{r} 80724 \\ +36168 \\ \hline \end{array}$	$\begin{array}{r} 47276 \\ +16505 \\ \hline \end{array}$	$\begin{array}{r} 375417 \\ +114659 \\ \hline \end{array}$
4.	$\begin{array}{r} 72464 \\ -57692 \\ \hline \end{array}$	$\begin{array}{r} 247392 \\ -\ 82643 \\ \hline \end{array}$	$\begin{array}{r} 920634 \\ -375023 \\ \hline \end{array}$	$\begin{array}{r} 723960 \\ -264637 \\ \hline \end{array}$
5.	$\begin{array}{r} 634172 \\ +265493 \\ \hline \end{array}$	$\begin{array}{r} 3176 \\ 8291 \\ +4793 \\ \hline \end{array}$	$\begin{array}{r} 86245 \\ 53792 \\ +20596 \\ \hline \end{array}$	$\begin{array}{r} 387464 \\ 722347 \\ +\ 18972 \\ \hline \end{array}$

Lesson 1.8 Problem Solving

Estimate the solution to each problem.

1. Paul weighs 287 pounds and Samuel weighs 145 pounds. Estimate the difference between the two boys' weights.

   Paul weighs about _____ pounds more than Samuel.

2. Mr. Williams earned 38,762 dollars last year and 52,335 dollars this year. Estimate how much Mr. Williams earned in two years.

   Mr. Williams earned about _____ dollars in two years.

3. The toy company ships out 3,452 dolls to Japan, 6,792 dolls to Spain, and 1,544 dolls to Canada annually. Estimate the number of dolls the toy company ships annually.

   The company ships about _____ dolls annually.

4. Attendance for two basketball games at the local college was 1,622 for the first game and 749 for the second game. Estimate the difference in attendance between the two games.

   About _____ more people attended the first game.

5. Kelly bought a large box of nails and a small box of nails. The large box contained 1,289 nails. The small box contained 468 nails. Estimate the difference between the large and small box.

   The large box contained about _____ more nails than the small box.

1.

2.

3.

4.

5.

Check What You Learned

Adding and Subtracting through 6 Digits

Add or subtract.

	a	b	c	d	e
1.	47 +36	12 +68	891 +456	128 +372	894 +206
2.	72 −41	61 −54	429 − 62	564 − 78	823 − 49
3.	263 +528	627 +745	4954 +1247	2436 +3475	5431 +2718
4.	847 −168	2147 − 136	6904 − 285	8762 − 783	3021 −1987
5.	5267 +8294	17645 +32347	39476 +22597	85233 +65987	49427 +36291
6.	46210 − 3704	74126 − 3214	93234 − 9487	654823 − 21754	312471 − 84536
7.	12592 +26439	364819 +176349	829 325 +467	4309 2617 +5173	11275 67548 +27634

Check What You Learned

Adding and Subtracting through 6 Digits

Circle Add or Subtract. Solve each problem.

8. Paul lives at the top of the hill, 3,276 steps from Henry's house. Continuing down the hill, Nick lives 6,989 steps past Henry. How many steps does Paul live from Nick?

Add   Subtract

Paul lives _____ steps from Nick.

8.

9. The hardware store has 6,545 five-inch screws and 7,158 two-inch screws. How many more two-inch screws than five-inch screws does the store have?

Add   Subtract

There are _____ more two-inch screws.

9.

10. Marta earned 6,148 tickets, Jack earned 3,359 tickets, and Susan earned 4,392 tickets. If they combine all their tickets, how many will there be?

Add   Subtract

Marta, Jack, and Susan have _____ tickets.

10.

11. Kendra is driving 105 miles to the beach. She has driven 37 miles. How many more miles does Kendra still have to drive?

Add   Subtract

Kendra must drive _____ more miles.

11.

12. The bakery produces 8,305 plain bagels, 2,856 onion bagels, 1,566 egg bagels, and 6,544 blueberry bagels daily. How many bagels does the bakery produce each day?

Add   Subtract

The bakery produces _____ bagels each day.

12.

Check What You Know

Multiplying through 4 Digits by 3 Digits

Multiply.

	a	b	c	d
1.	48 × 7	64 × 3	235 × 5	829 × 8
2.	3146 × 2	7402 × 3	21 ×55	72 ×94
3.	49 ×35	380 × 22	816 × 32	276 × 80
4.	2714 × 52	5216 × 16	177 ×402	818 ×321
5.	445 ×176	3420 × 634	5867 × 382	6334 × 257

Check What You Know

SHOW YOUR WORK

Multiplying through 4 Digits by 3 Digits

Solve each problem.

6. Tyrone practices baseball 2 hours a day, 4 days a week. How many hours does Tyrone practice baseball each week?

Tyrone practices _____ hours each week.

7. Alfonso studied for his science test 3 hours a day for 22 days. How many hours did Alfonso study in all?

Alfonso studied for _____ hours.

8. The symphony has 34 performances scheduled this year. There are 527 tickets available for each performance. If all the seats are filled for each performance, how many tickets will the symphony have sold?

The symphony will have sold _____ tickets.

9. Century High School is having a bake sale for the community. Each person is required to bring in 12 baked goods. If there are 2,537 students enrolled in the school, how many baked goods will there be for sale?

There will be _____ baked goods for sale.

10. If a restaurant serves 336 customers a day, 210 days a year, how many customers will the restaurant serve in a year?

The restaurant will serve _____ customers in a year.

6.	7.
8.	**9.**
10.	

Lesson 2.1 Multiplying 1, 2, and 3 Digits by 1 Digit

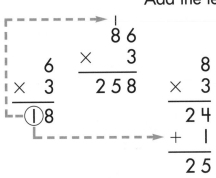

Multiply
6 by 3.

Multiply
8 by 3.
Add the tens.

Multiply
2 by 8.

Multiply
3 by 8.
Add 1 ten.

Multiply
5 by 8.
Add 2
hundreds.

Multiply.

	a	b	c	d	e	f
1.	6 ×3	8 ×2	4 ×7	22 × 9	17 × 6	42 × 7
2.	74 × 6	34 × 9	28 × 6	163 × 1	317 × 4	265 × 5
3.	836 × 4	627 × 8	352 × 2	73 × 7	65 × 9	87 × 2
4.	26 × 5	84 × 8	92 × 3	258 × 4	736 × 8	949 × 6
5.	705 × 5	146 × 7	628 × 9	37 × 2	97 × 1	52 × 4
6.	916 × 5	276 × 2	473 × 3	356 × 8	575 × 4	293 × 6

Lesson 2.2 Multiplying 2 and 3 Digits by 2 Digits

Multiply right to left.

If 24 × 3 = 72, then 24 × 30 = 720.

Multiply right to left.

$$
\begin{array}{r}
\overset{2}{2}4 \\
\times\ \ 7 \\
\hline
168
\end{array}
$$

$$
\begin{array}{r}
24 \\
\times\ 37 \\
\hline
168 \\
+720 \\
\hline
888
\end{array}
$$

$$
\begin{array}{r}
\overset{1}{2}4 \\
\times\ 30 \\
\hline
720
\end{array}
$$

$$
\begin{array}{r}
427 \\
\times\ \ 1 \\
\hline
427
\end{array}
$$

$$
\begin{array}{r}
427 \\
\times\ \ \ 61 \\
\hline
427 \\
+25620 \\
\hline
26047
\end{array}
$$

$$
\begin{array}{r}
427 \\
\times\ \ \ 60 \\
\hline
25620
\end{array}
$$

Multiply.

	a	b	c	d	e	f
1.	43 ×42	75 ×12	52 ×28	36 ×91	16 ×77	21 ×13
2.	24 ×87	62 ×54	96 ×32	18 ×47	33 ×79	45 ×63
3.	26 ×53	39 ×74	44 ×81	473 × 64	856 × 22	375 × 49
4.	838 × 58	266 × 93	372 × 46	659 × 78	428 × 37	235 × 86
5.	907 × 33	415 × 27	364 × 82	547 × 54	739 × 62	697 × 76

Lesson 2.3 Problem Solving

Solve each problem.

1. Mr. Benson must order 32 calculators for each fifth grade class. There are 6 classes. How many calculators must Mr. Benson order?

   Each class needs _____ calculators.

   There are _____ classes.

   Mr. Benson must order _____ calculators.

2. It takes Rosa 173 minutes to knit a scarf. How many minutes will it take her to knit 4 scarves.

   It takes Rosa _____ minutes to knit a scarf.

   She wants to knit _____ scarves.

   It will take Rosa _____ minutes.

3. There are 24 hours in one day. How many hours are there in 18 days?

   There are _____ hours in a day.

   There are _____ hours in 18 days.

4. It takes 47 apples to fill a bushel. There are 24 bushels to fill. How many apples does the farmer need to fill all the bushels?

   There are _____ apples in a bushel.

   There are _____ bushels to fill.

   The farmer needs _____ apples to fill all the bushels.

5. Bob's car can go 23 miles on one gallon of gas. The gas tank holds 26 gallons. How many miles can Bob's car go on a full tank of gas?

   Bob's car can go _____ miles on one gallon of gas.

   The car holds _____ gallons of gas.

   It can go _____ miles on a full tank of gas.

1.	
2.	3.
4.	5.

Lesson 2.4 Multiplying 4 Digits by 1 and 2 Digits

Multiply from right to left.

$2 \times 7 = 14 + 2 = \textcircled{1}6$
$3 \times 7 = 21 + 1 = 22$

$\begin{array}{r} 1\ 2\ 4 \\ 3\ 2\ 3\ 6 \\ \times \quad\ \ 7 \\ \hline 2\ 2\ 6\ 5\ 2 \end{array}$

$6 \times 7 = \textcircled{4}2$
$3 \times 7 = 21 + 4 = \textcircled{2}5$

$\begin{array}{r} 7\ 1\ 9\ 8 \\ \times \quad\ 1\ 4 \\ \hline 2\ 8\ 7\ 9\ 2 \\ +\ 7\ 1\ 9\ 8\ 0 \\ \hline 1\ 0\ 0\ 7\ 7\ 2 \end{array}$

$\begin{array}{r} 7\ 1\ 9\ 8 \\ \times \quad\ \ 4 \\ \hline 2\ 8\ 7\ 9\ 2 \end{array}$

$\begin{array}{r} 7\ 1\ 9\ 8 \\ \times \quad\ 1\ 0 \\ \hline 7\ 1\ 9\ 8\ 0 \end{array}$

If $7198 \times 1 = 7198$,
then
$7198 \times 10 = 71980$.

Multiply.

	a	b	c	d	e
1.	$\begin{array}{r} 2763 \\ \times\ \ \ 5 \\ \hline \end{array}$	$\begin{array}{r} 6204 \\ \times\ \ \ 7 \\ \hline \end{array}$	$\begin{array}{r} 3221 \\ \times\ \ \ 4 \\ \hline \end{array}$	$\begin{array}{r} 8634 \\ \times\ \ \ 8 \\ \hline \end{array}$	$\begin{array}{r} 7253 \\ \times\ \ \ 6 \\ \hline \end{array}$
2.	$\begin{array}{r} 4728 \\ \times\ \ \ 4 \\ \hline \end{array}$	$\begin{array}{r} 3962 \\ \times\ \ \ 9 \\ \hline \end{array}$	$\begin{array}{r} 1854 \\ \times\ \ \ 2 \\ \hline \end{array}$	$\begin{array}{r} 5273 \\ \times\ \ \ 6 \\ \hline \end{array}$	$\begin{array}{r} 4456 \\ \times\ \ \ 3 \\ \hline \end{array}$
3.	$\begin{array}{r} 7526 \\ \times\ \ \ 3 \\ \hline \end{array}$	$\begin{array}{r} 9428 \\ \times\ \ \ 2 \\ \hline \end{array}$	$\begin{array}{r} 3725 \\ \times\ \ 28 \\ \hline \end{array}$	$\begin{array}{r} 6414 \\ \times\ \ 37 \\ \hline \end{array}$	$\begin{array}{r} 2889 \\ \times\ \ 41 \\ \hline \end{array}$
4.	$\begin{array}{r} 5297 \\ \times\ \ 64 \\ \hline \end{array}$	$\begin{array}{r} 4175 \\ \times\ \ 23 \\ \hline \end{array}$	$\begin{array}{r} 8052 \\ \times\ \ 46 \\ \hline \end{array}$	$\begin{array}{r} 2988 \\ \times\ \ 85 \\ \hline \end{array}$	$\begin{array}{r} 6364 \\ \times\ \ 92 \\ \hline \end{array}$
5.	$\begin{array}{r} 3562 \\ \times\ \ 27 \\ \hline \end{array}$	$\begin{array}{r} 7451 \\ \times\ \ 54 \\ \hline \end{array}$	$\begin{array}{r} 1920 \\ \times\ \ 83 \\ \hline \end{array}$	$\begin{array}{r} 9163 \\ \times\ \ 72 \\ \hline \end{array}$	$\begin{array}{r} 4276 \\ \times\ \ 56 \\ \hline \end{array}$

Lesson 2.5 Multiplying 3 and 4 Digits by 3 Digits

```
  524        524              524                                          2276
×   1     ×  481          ×    80         2276        2276           ×      90
  524 ----→  524          ---41920      ×    4     ×   394          --204840
           41920                         9104 ----→ 9104                204840
         +209600 ←                                 204840 ←
          252044                524     +682800 ←                        2276
                             ×  400      896744                      ×    300
                             --209600                               --682800
```

If 524 × 8 = 4192, then 524 × 80 = 41920.   If 2276 × 9 = 20484, then 2276 × 90 = 204840.
If 524 × 4 = 2096, then 524 × 400 = 209600.   If 2276 × 3 = 6828, then 2276 × 300 = 682800.

Multiply.

	a	b	c	d
1.	273 ×421	144 ×672	906 ×218	364 ×725
2.	531 ×573	837 ×391	476 ×152	259 ×632
3.	782 ×443	685 ×194	2176 × 328	4608 × 742
4.	1554 × 269	2137 × 528	5736 × 471	6193 × 346
5.	3245 × 822	9764 × 253	7240 × 294	3827 × 153

Lesson 2.6 — Multiplication Practice

Multiply.

	a	b	c	d
1.	26 × 5	57 × 3	423 × 2	716 × 8
2.	3142 × 5	6271 × 7	8409 × 6	48 ×75
3.	62 ×38	284 × 29	615 × 42	384 × 52
4.	2865 × 31	7523 × 52	5323 × 81	239 ×433
5.	732 ×328	291 ×625	1472 × 563	3194 × 850

Lesson 2.7 Estimating Products

Round each number to its highest place value.

$$
\begin{array}{r}
3764 \longrightarrow 4000 \\
\times\ 247 \longrightarrow \times 200 \\
\hline
800000
\end{array}
$$

$4 \times 2 = 8$ $40 \times 2 = 80$
$4 \times 20 = 80$ $400 \times 20 = 8000$
$4 \times 200 = 800$ $4000 \times 200 = 800000$

Estimate the product.

	a	b	c	d	e
1.	76 ×2	38 ×5	21 ×9	461 ×3	728 ×4
2.	115 ×3	983 ×8	3214 ×6	5789 ×7	8365 ×9
3.	56 ×32	89 ×25	41 ×27	95 ×63	75 ×18
4.	294 ×51	729 ×44	129 ×37	381 ×23	897 ×68
5.	3751 ×72	5242 ×25	1803 ×61	4395 ×76	9178 ×39
6.	218 ×924	807 ×463	835 ×194	431 ×728	648 ×599
7.	5130 ×626	4767 ×325	9543 ×689	9300 ×862	6827 ×423

Lesson 2.8 Problem Solving

Solve each problem.

1. On Monday, the amusement park offered tickets for 9 dollars. On that day, 2,068 people bought tickets for the park. How much money did the park make on ticket sales that day?

   The amusement park made _____ dollars on Monday.

2. Mr. Tao taught mathematics to classes of 37 students for 27 years. How many students has Mr. Tao taught in all?

   Mr. Tao has taught _____ students.

3. If Latisha brushes her teeth 14 times a week, how many times will Latisha have brushed her teeth in 107 weeks?

   Latisha will have brushed her teeth _____ times.

4. Florence recently opened 29 candle shops. In each shop, she stocked 3,165 candles. How many candles has Florence stocked in all the shops?

   Florence has stocked _____ candles in all.

5. There are 24 movie frames for one second of film. There are 7,238 seconds in a movie. How many frames are there total for the whole movie?

   There are _____ movie frames.

6. Harmony Corporation planted 114 trees in 428 cities across the United States. How many total trees did Harmony Corporation plant?

   Harmony Corporation planted _____ trees.

1.	
2.	3.
4.	5.
6.	

Check What You Learned

Multiplying through 4 Digits by 3 Digits

Multiply.

	a	b	c	d
1.	45 ×7	862 ×9	328 ×5	2476 ×6
2.	25 ×13	59 ×32	280 ×93	814 ×37
3.	497 ×48	6492 ×82	2158 ×32	8291 ×54
4.	212 ×561	394 ×627	875 ×169	250 ×937
5.	4176 ×283	9192 ×562	7315 ×141	5639 ×374

Check What You Learned

Multiplying through 4 Digits by 3 Digits

Solve each problem.

6. The hardware store contains 56 shelves with paint. There are 32 cans of paint on each shelf. How many total cans of paint are there?

There are _____ total cans of paint.

6.

7. If the library loans 726 books a day, how many books will the library have loaned after 21 days?

The library will have loaned _____ books.

7.

8. The factory produces 274 sweaters in a day. How many sweaters will it produce in 259 days?

The factory will produce _____ sweaters.

8.

9. A freight train carries 7,153 boxes of soap. Each box weighs 44 pounds. How many pounds of soap is the train carrying?

The train is carrying _____ pounds of soap.

9.

10. The Haws Corporation has 452 employees. Each employee works 1,705 hours a year. What are the total number of employee hours a year for the Haws Corporation.

There are _____ employee hours a year.

10.

Check What You Know

Dividing through 5 Digits by 2 Digits

Divide.

	a	b	c	d
1.	3)762	7)423	6)1758	4)8294
2.	8)34088	5)24716	12)84	17)51
3.	21)74	14)39	72)216	33)594
4.	24)671	63)887	45)6075	89)5784
5.	53)3299	92)8147	14)33152	76)26477

NAME _____

Check What You Know

Dividing through 5 Digits by 2 Digits

Solve each problem.

6. A restaurant has 245 seats with 5 seats at each table. How many tables does the restaurant have?

   The restaurant has _____ tables.

7. Homer buys 3 newspapers every week. If Homer has 627 newspapers, how many weeks has he been buying them?

   He has been buying newspapers for _____ weeks.

8. A group of 6 children started a lawn mowing company at the beginning of the summer. At the end of the summer, the company had mowed 486 lawns. How many lawns did each child mow if each mowed an equal number?

   Each child mowed _____ lawns.

9. The Wilkinson family drove 1,374 miles in 9 days. How many miles did the Wilkinsons drive each day if they drove the same amount? How many more miles did they drive on the last day?

   The Wilkinson family drove _____ miles each day.

   They drove _____ extra miles on the last day.

10. Alfredo waited in 13 lines at the amusement park for a total of 325 minutes. Alfredo stood in each line for the same amount of time. How many minutes did he stand in each line?

    Alfredo stood in each line for _____ minutes.

11. Mrs. Hawkins must split a group of 252 students into groups of 22 for the school field trip. How many students will be in each group?

    There will be _____ students in each group.

    There will be _____ extra students.

6.	7.
8.	9.
10.	11.

Lesson 3.1 Dividing 1 and 2 Digits by 1 Digit

$$
\begin{array}{r}
4 \leftarrow \text{quotient} \\
\text{divisor} \longrightarrow 8\overline{)3\,2} \leftarrow \text{dividend} \\
-3\,2 \\
\hline
0
\end{array}
$$

$8 \times 4 = 32$

So, $32 \div 8 = 4$.

Divide.

	a	b	c	d	e	f
1.	3)9	2)4	3)6	4)8	1)7	1)9
2.	3)0	2)10	7)14	2)6	3)54	3)3
3.	1)5	3)12	6)12	2)2	5)10	4)12
4.	5)25	4)16	3)15	8)72	2)22	3)21
5.	8)24	4)12	6)54	8)40	4)36	4)20
6.	4)28	4)4	3)18	6)18	9)63	6)36
7.	7)63	3)27	4)32	8)64	8)48	9)18
8.	4)24	9)72	8)32	5)20	9)45	6)30
9.	6)24	7)49	9)81	5)30	3)21	5)15
10.	8)16	2)8	7)28	7)42	6)48	5)35

Lesson 3.2   Dividing 2 and 3 Digits by 1 Digit

divisor   dividend

$$5 \div 3 = 1 \text{ remainder } 2$$
$$22 \div 3 = 7 \text{ remainder } 1$$
$$18 \div 3 = 6 \text{ remainder } 0$$

$$\begin{array}{r} 1 \\ 3\overline{)528} \end{array}$$

subtract $\{$ $\begin{array}{r} -3 \\ \hline 22 \end{array}$

$$\begin{array}{r} 17 \\ 3\overline{)528} \end{array}$$
subtract $\{$ $\begin{array}{r} -3 \\ \hline 22 \end{array}$
subtract $\{$ $\begin{array}{r} -21 \\ \hline 18 \end{array}$

$$\begin{array}{r} 176 \leftarrow \text{ quotient} \\ 3\overline{)528} \end{array}$$
$\begin{array}{r} -3 \\ \hline 22 \end{array}$
$\begin{array}{r} -21 \\ \hline 18 \end{array}$
subtract $\{$ $\begin{array}{r} -18 \\ \hline 0 \leftarrow \text{ remainder} = 0 \end{array}$

Divide.

	a	b	c	d	e
1.	$4\overline{)42}$	$8\overline{)67}$	$6\overline{)51}$	$3\overline{)25}$	$9\overline{)82}$
2.	$5\overline{)82}$	$6\overline{)77}$	$4\overline{)99}$	$2\overline{)34}$	$7\overline{)44}$
3.	$6\overline{)132}$	$9\overline{)374}$	$4\overline{)849}$	$5\overline{)757}$	$3\overline{)216}$
4.	$2\overline{)875}$	$6\overline{)461}$	$8\overline{)639}$	$7\overline{)323}$	$4\overline{)572}$

Lesson 3.3 Dividing 3 and 4 Digits by 1 Digit

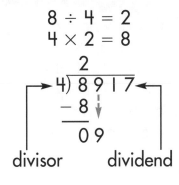

$8 \div 4 = 2$
$4 \times 2 = 8$

```
      2
  4)8917
   -8
    09
```
divisor   dividend

$9 \div 4 = 2$
remainder 1

```
     22
  4)8917
   -8
    09
   -8
    11
```

$11 \div 4 = 2$
remainder 3

```
     222
  4)8917
   -8
    09
   -8
    11
   -8
    37
```

$37 \div 4 = 9$
remainder 1

```
     2229  ← quotient
  4)8917
   -8
    09
   -8
    11
   -8
    37
   -36
     1  ← remainder
```

Divide.

	a	b	c	d
1.	3)650	6)925	8)487	2)234
2.	7)496	4)568	7)1426	3)3746
3.	5)8503	9)6292	4)3166	2)2317

Lesson 3.4   Estimating Quotients

$7)\overline{24}$ Think of what you can round the dividend (24) to so that it is easy to mentally divide by the divisor (7). The quotient is 3.

3
$7)\overline{21}$
-21
$\overline{0}$

$5)\overline{378}$ Think of what you can round the dividend (378) to so that it is easy to mentally divide by the divisor (5).

quotient ⟶ 76
$5)\overline{380}$
$-35↓$
$\overline{30}$
-30
$\overline{0}$

Estimate each quotient.

	a	b	c	d
1.	$3)\overline{16}$	$7)\overline{36}$	$3)\overline{74}$	$4)\overline{83}$
2.	$4)\overline{27}$	$6)\overline{217}$	$8)\overline{481}$	$7)\overline{764}$
3.	$9)\overline{362}$	$2)\overline{563}$	$4)\overline{1378}$	$3)\overline{4269}$
4.	$8)\overline{2448}$	$5)\overline{9216}$	$9)\overline{3502}$	$5)\overline{7358}$

Lesson 3.5   Dividing 2 Digits by 2 Digits

$$
\begin{array}{r}
4 \\
19\overline{)78} \\
-76 \\
\hline
2 \\
\end{array}
$$
$19 \times 4 = 76$
$78 - 76 = 2$

$$
\begin{array}{r}
4 \ r\ 2 \\
19\overline{)78} \\
-76 \\
\hline
②
\end{array}
$$

The quotient is 4.
The remainder is 2.

Divide.

	a	b	c	d
1.	$16\overline{)34}$	$13\overline{)72}$	$28\overline{)56}$	$19\overline{)49}$
2.	$21\overline{)78}$	$11\overline{)43}$	$12\overline{)97}$	$17\overline{)64}$
3.	$18\overline{)25}$	$29\overline{)87}$	$13\overline{)39}$	$35\overline{)77}$
4.	$21\overline{)63}$	$37\overline{)92}$	$14\overline{)53}$	$26\overline{)83}$

Lesson 3.6   Dividing 3 Digits by 2 Digits

$71 \div 14 = 5$
remainder 1

$18 \div 14 = 1$
remainder 4

$$14 \times 5 = 70 \dashrightarrow \begin{array}{r} 5 \\ 14\overline{)718} \\ -70\downarrow \\ \hline 18 \end{array}$$

$$\begin{array}{r} 51 \\ 14\overline{)718} \\ -70\downarrow \\ \hline 18 \\ -14 \\ \hline 4 \end{array}$$

$$\begin{array}{r} 51 \; r4 \\ 14\overline{)718} \\ -70\downarrow \\ \hline 18 \\ -14 \\ \hline \textcircled{4} \end{array}$$

The quotient is 51.
The remainder is 4.

Divide.

	a	b	c	d
1.	$23\overline{)264}$	$32\overline{)571}$	$81\overline{)724}$	$52\overline{)328}$
2.	$61\overline{)488}$	$35\overline{)175}$	$82\overline{)362}$	$47\overline{)719}$
3.	$97\overline{)891}$	$26\overline{)423}$	$43\overline{)916}$	$57\overline{)649}$

Lesson 3.7 Dividing 4 Digits by 2 Digits

$$51 \div 23 = 2 \quad 57 \div 23 = 2 \quad 113 \div 23 = 4$$
$$\text{remainder } 5 \quad \text{remainder } 11 \quad \text{remainder } 21$$

$$
\begin{array}{r}
2 \\
23{\overline{\smash{\big)}\,5173}} \\
-46 \\
\hline
5
\end{array}
\qquad
\begin{array}{r}
22 \\
23{\overline{\smash{\big)}\,5173}} \\
-46 \\
\hline
57 \\
-46 \\
\hline
113
\end{array}
\qquad
\begin{array}{r}
224 \\
23{\overline{\smash{\big)}\,5173}} \\
-46 \\
\hline
57 \\
-46 \\
\hline
113 \\
-92 \\
\hline
21
\end{array}
\qquad
\begin{array}{r}
224\ \text{r}21 \\
23{\overline{\smash{\big)}\,5173}} \\
-46 \\
\hline
57 \\
-46 \\
\hline
113 \\
-92 \\
\hline
21
\end{array}
$$

$23 \times 2 = 46$

$23 \times 2 = 46$

$23 \times 4 = 92$

The quotient is 224.
The remainder is 21.

Divide.

	a	b	c	d
1.	43)6571	22)8294	62)3628	88)4773
2.	56)2829	89)5340	75)8195	29)4872
3.	63)1890	31)6263	96)5379	48)7246

Lesson 3.8   Dividing 5 Digits by 2 Digits

$$
\begin{array}{r}
1 \\
75\overline{)81724} \\
-75\downarrow \\
\hline
67
\end{array}
$$

$$
\begin{array}{r}
10 \\
75\overline{)81724} \\
-75\downarrow \\
\hline
67 \\
-0\downarrow \\
\hline
672
\end{array}
$$

$$
\begin{array}{r}
108 \\
75\overline{)81724} \\
-75 \\
\hline
67 \\
-0 \\
\hline
672 \\
-600 \\
\hline
724
\end{array}
$$

$$
\begin{array}{r}
1089\ r49 \\
75\overline{)81724} \\
-75 \\
\hline
67 \\
-0 \\
\hline
672 \\
-600 \\
\hline
724 \\
-675 \\
\hline
\boxed{49}
\end{array}
$$

$75 \times 1 = 75$
$81 \div 75 = 1$
remainder 6

$67 \div 75 = 0$
remainder 67

$672 \div 75 = 8$
remainder 72

$724 \div 75 = 9$
remainder 49

Divide.

	a	b	c	d
1.	$21\overline{)37654}$	$45\overline{)73425}$	$64\overline{)21760}$	$86\overline{)90427}$
2.	$51\overline{)45951}$	$24\overline{)69329}$	$92\overline{)77562}$	$39\overline{)32869}$

Lesson 3.9   Division Practice

Divide.

	a	b	c	d

1. 4)3726   7)5943   5)61425   9)81472

2. 12)77   26)54   49)81   32)468

3. 56)988   85)267   76)1547   98)6822

4. 67)4631   71)32196   42)53447   59)81748

Lesson 3.10 Problem Solving

SHOW YOUR WORK

Solve each problem.

1. Jamal can swim 56 feet in one minute. If Jamal swims 784 feet, how many minutes does he swim?	**1.**
Jamal can swim _____ feet in one minute.	
Jamal swims _____ feet.	
Jamal swims for _____ minutes.	
2. Eighteen employees worked the same number of hours on Tuesday. The company calculated 126 employee hours for that day. How many hours did each employee work?	**2.**
There were _____ employees at work.	
All 18 employees worked _____ hours.	
Each employee worked _____ hours.	
3. The concert manager needed to figure the number of seats in each section of the concert hall. If there are 3,615 seats in the concert hall and there are 15 different sections, how many seats are there in each section?	**3.**
There are _____ seats in the concert hall.	
There are _____ different sections of seating.	
There are _____ seats in each section.	
4. A cosmetic company is passing out free samples of a new product. They started with 618 samples and passed them out to 87 houses. If each house received the same number of samples, how many samples did each house receive from the cosmetic company? How many samples were left over?	**4.**
The cosmetic company started with _____ samples.	
The company visited _____ houses.	
Each house received _____ samples.	
There were _____ samples left over.	

Check What You Learned

Dividing through 5 Digits by 2 Digits

Divide.

	a	b	c	d
1.	6)2142	4)8676	9)65376	3)76214
2.	12)72	27)64	35)93	18)58
3.	49)392	34)589	72)745	45)213
4.	61)1708	94)4649	52)9243	68)3174
5.	16)42368	81)27488	24)86916	77)53476

Check What You Learned

Dividing through 5 Digits by 2 Digits

Solve each problem.

6. Rita's mom purchased 126 balloons for Rita's birthday party. If each group has 7 balloons, how many groups of balloons did Rita's mom put together?

   There are _____ groups of balloons.

7. Carlos worked 1,784 hours in a year. If Carlos worked 8 hours each day, how many days did Carlos work during the year?

   Carlos worked _____ days during the year.

8. Seabreeze Travel Agency planned trips for 5,275 people in February. If 5 people are going on each trip, how many trips were planned by Seabreeze during the month of February?

   Seabreeze Travel Agency planned _____ trips.

9. Patty wants to make 14 apple pies. She picked 107 apples. How many apples will be in each pie? How many apples will be left over?

   There will be _____ apples in each pie.

   There will be _____ apples left over.

10. Ms. Santos has 4,286 inches of fabric. She needs 32 inches for a sleeve. How many sleeves can Ms. San Gabriel make? How many inches of fabric will be left over?

    Ms. Santos can make _____ sleeves.

    There will be _____ inches of fabric left over.

11. Mary is organizing her stamps in a book. She has collected 23,754 stamps. She is planning to put 37 stamps on each page. How many pages long will her stamp book be?

    Mary's stamp book will be _____ pages long.

6.	7.
8.	9.
10.	11.

CHAPTER 3 POSTTEST

Check What You Know

Understanding Fractions

Label each number as prime or composite.

	a	b	c
1.	17 _____	21 _____	77 _____
2.	82 _____	51 _____	25 _____

Find the greatest common factor for each set of numbers.

3.	18 and 22	25 and 50	54 and 36
	_____	_____	_____
4.	40 and 8	16, 24, and 18	32, 8, and 40
	_____	_____	_____

Write out the prime factorization for each number.

5.	6 _____	21 _____	12 _____
6.	25 _____	32 _____	44 _____

Reduce each fraction to simplest form.

7.	$\frac{6}{9}$ _____	$\frac{12}{36}$ _____	$\frac{20}{32}$ _____
8.	$\frac{21}{49}$ _____	$\frac{15}{18}$ _____	$\frac{40}{45}$ _____
9.	$\frac{12}{14}$ _____	$\frac{19}{38}$ _____	$\frac{27}{30}$ _____

NAME _____

 Check What You Know

Understanding Fractions

Write each improper fraction as a mixed numeral in simplest form.

	a	b	c
10.	$\frac{10}{7}$ _____	$\frac{25}{3}$ _____	$\frac{48}{21}$ _____
11.	$\frac{46}{36}$ _____	$\frac{30}{7}$ _____	$\frac{22}{8}$ _____

Write each mixed numeral as an improper fraction.

12.	$2\frac{3}{4}$ _____	$6\frac{8}{9}$ _____	$8\frac{11}{12}$ _____
13.	$4\frac{4}{9}$ _____	$5\frac{2}{7}$ _____	$3\frac{3}{5}$ _____

Write each mixed numeral in simplest form.

14.	$5\frac{3}{6}$ _____	$2\frac{8}{3}$ _____	$7\frac{9}{4}$ _____
15.	$7\frac{12}{5}$ _____	$3\frac{8}{12}$ _____	$2\frac{7}{4}$ _____

Lesson 4.1 Numerator and Denominator

 $\frac{1}{6}$ of the picture is shaded.

$$\frac{1}{6} \longleftarrow \text{numerator}$$

$$\text{denominator} \longrightarrow \frac{1}{6}$$

$$\frac{1}{6} = \text{one-sixth}$$

Write a fraction for each of the following.

	a		**b**	
1.	two-sevenths	_____	three-fourths	_____
2.	one-ninth	_____	three-fifths	_____
3.	seven-eighths	_____	nine-tenths	_____

Write each fraction in words.

4. $\frac{7}{9}$ _____ $\frac{1}{4}$ _____

5. $\frac{3}{10}$ _____ $\frac{5}{6}$ _____

Write a fraction for the shaded regions in simplest form.

6. _____   _____

7. 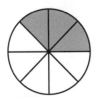 _____    _____

Lesson 4.2 Prime and Composite Numbers

A number is called **prime** if its only factors are 1 and itself.

For example, 7 is a prime number. The only factors of 7 are 1 and 7.

A number is called **composite** if it has more than two factors.

For example, 8 is a composite number. 1, 2, 4, and 8 are all factors of 8.

A composite number can be written as the product of prime numbers. This is called **prime factorization** of a number.

$8 = 2 \times 2 \times 2$

Label each number as prime or composite.

	a		b	
1.	64 _____		22 _____	
2.	43 _____		36 _____	
3.	53 _____		89 _____	
4.	72 _____		31 _____	
5.	19 _____		93 _____	
6.	48 _____		75 _____	

Write out the prime factorization for each number.

7.	32 _____		78 _____	
8.	74 _____		18 _____	
9.	96 _____		55 _____	
10.	38 _____		24 _____	
11.	27 _____		63 _____	
12.	51 _____		88 _____	

Lesson 4.3   Finding the Greatest Common Factor

The **greatest common factor** of two or more numbers is the largest factor they have in common.

A **factor** is a number that divides evenly (no remainder) into a given number.

A **common factor** of two or more numbers is a number that divides each of the given numbers evenly.

16, 24, and 36

The factors of 16 are 1, 2, 4, 8, and 16.

The factors of 24 are 1, 2, 3, 4, 6, 8, 12, and 24.

The factors of 36 are 1, 2, 3, 4, 6, 9, 18, and 36.

2 and 4 are common factors of 16, 24, and 36.

The greatest common factor of 16, 24, and 36 is 4.

Find the greatest common factor for each set of numbers.

	a		b	
1.	14 and 42	_____	27 and 18	_____
2.	36 and 24	_____	45 and 20	_____
3.	72 and 54	_____	42 and 49	_____
4.	86 and 94	_____	66 and 11	_____
5.	52 and 26	_____	12 and 40	_____
6.	9, 12, and 21	_____	16, 32, and 64	_____
7.	15, 25, and 40	_____	27, 36, and 72	_____

Lesson 4.4   Reducing Fractions to their Simplest Form

$$\frac{12 \div 4}{16 \div 4} = \frac{3}{4} \qquad \frac{12}{16} = \frac{3}{4}$$

To reduce a fraction to its simplest form, divide the numerator and denominator by the same number. The fraction is in simplest form when 1 is the only common factor.

$$\frac{36 \div 36}{72 \div 36} = \frac{1}{2} \qquad \frac{36}{72} = \frac{1}{2}$$

Reduce each fraction to simplest form.

	a	b	c
1.	$\frac{3}{6}$ _____	$\frac{5}{10}$ _____	$\frac{9}{18}$ _____
2.	$\frac{6}{24}$ _____	$\frac{4}{12}$ _____	$\frac{2}{10}$ _____
3.	$\frac{4}{20}$ _____	$\frac{12}{15}$ _____	$\frac{8}{32}$ _____
4.	$\frac{18}{36}$ _____	$\frac{26}{28}$ _____	$\frac{17}{68}$ _____
5.	$\frac{25}{35}$ _____	$\frac{51}{75}$ _____	$\frac{28}{36}$ _____
6.	$\frac{22}{64}$ _____	$\frac{49}{63}$ _____	$\frac{24}{96}$ _____

Lesson 4.5 Changing Improper Fractions to Mixed Numerals

$\dfrac{13}{6}$ means $13 \div 6$ or $6\overline{)13}$

$$\begin{array}{r} 2\frac{1}{6} \\ 6\overline{)13} \\ -12 \\ \hline 1 \end{array}$$

$1 \longrightarrow 1 \div 6 = \boxed{\tfrac{1}{6}}$

So, $\dfrac{13}{6} = 2\dfrac{1}{6}$

$\dfrac{13}{6}$ is an **improper fraction**, meaning the denominator divides the numerator at least one time. In other words, the numerator is greater than the denominator.

$2\dfrac{1}{6}$ is a **mixed numeral**. This is the simplest form of an improper fraction.

Write each improper fraction as a mixed numeral in simplest form.

	a	b	c
1.	$\dfrac{5}{3}$ _____	$\dfrac{7}{6}$ _____	$\dfrac{9}{5}$ _____
2.	$\dfrac{3}{2}$ _____	$\dfrac{4}{3}$ _____	$\dfrac{8}{5}$ _____
3.	$\dfrac{7}{5}$ _____	$\dfrac{9}{7}$ _____	$\dfrac{5}{4}$ _____
4.	$\dfrac{32}{6}$ _____	$\dfrac{51}{4}$ _____	$\dfrac{49}{9}$ _____
5.	$\dfrac{66}{5}$ _____	$\dfrac{83}{3}$ _____	$\dfrac{28}{5}$ _____
6.	$\dfrac{29}{3}$ _____	$\dfrac{38}{7}$ _____	$\dfrac{64}{6}$ _____

Lesson 4.6   Working with Mixed Numerals

A **mixed numeral** is a whole number plus a proper fraction.

To change a mixed numeral to an improper fraction, multiply the whole number by the denominator and add the numerator. Use the same denominator.

$$4\frac{2}{3} = \frac{(4 \times 3) + 2}{3} = \frac{12 + 2}{3} = \frac{14}{3}$$

$\frac{14}{3}$ is the mixed numeral of the improper fraction $4\frac{2}{3}$.

A mixed numeral is in simplest form when the fraction is in simplest form and names a number less than 1.

$$6\frac{8}{12} = 6 + \frac{8}{12} = 6 + \frac{8 \div 4}{12 \div 4} = 6\frac{2}{3}$$

$$3\frac{10}{4} = 3 + \frac{10}{4} = 3 + \frac{10 \div 2}{4 \div 2} = 3 + \frac{5}{2} = 3 + 2\frac{1}{2} = 5\frac{1}{2}$$

Write each mixed numeral as an improper fraction.

	a	b	c	d	e
1.	$8\frac{2}{3}$ ____	$6\frac{7}{8}$ ____	$9\frac{1}{2}$ ____	$5\frac{4}{7}$ ____	$1\frac{5}{7}$ ____
2.	$8\frac{11}{13}$ ____	$2\frac{5}{12}$ ____	$3\frac{5}{16}$ ____	$1\frac{11}{6}$ ____	$6\frac{12}{8}$ ____

Write each mixed numeral in simplest form.

3.	$2\frac{6}{8}$ ____	$4\frac{5}{10}$ ____	$8\frac{2}{6}$ ____	$5\frac{3}{9}$ ____	$3\frac{9}{12}$ ____
4.	$4\frac{9}{15}$ ____	$7\frac{8}{24}$ ____	$2\frac{4}{10}$ ____	$5\frac{9}{7}$ ____	$6\frac{9}{4}$ ____

Check What You Learned

Understanding Fractions

Label each number as prime or composite.

	a		b
I.	27 _____	29	_____
2.	41 _____	52	_____

Find the greatest common factor for each set of numbers.

3.   10 and 15   14 and 28

_____   _____

4.   20 and 18   64 and 48

_____   _____

Write out the prime factorization for each number.

5.   64 _____   51 _____

Reduce each fraction to simplest form.

6. $\dfrac{6}{9}$ _____ $\dfrac{12}{36}$ _____

7. $\dfrac{20}{32}$ _____ $\dfrac{21}{49}$ _____

8. $\dfrac{15}{18}$ _____ $\dfrac{40}{45}$ _____

9. $\dfrac{8}{16}$ _____ $\dfrac{48}{54}$ _____

Check What You Learned

Understanding Fractions

Write each improper fraction as a mixed numeral in simplest form.

	a	b	c
10.	$\frac{22}{4}$ _____	$\frac{9}{8}$ _____	$\frac{17}{6}$ _____
11.	$\frac{23}{9}$ _____	$\frac{26}{12}$ _____	$\frac{13}{12}$ _____
12.	$\frac{18}{4}$ _____	$\frac{17}{12}$ _____	$\frac{84}{7}$ _____
13.	$\frac{37}{6}$ _____	$\frac{49}{9}$ _____	$\frac{50}{8}$ _____

Write each mixed numeral or improper fraction in simplest form.

	a	b	c
14.	$3\frac{6}{8}$ _____	$9\frac{8}{12}$ _____	$4\frac{7}{14}$ _____
15.	$6\frac{8}{3}$ _____	$2\frac{9}{6}$ _____	$5\frac{12}{10}$ _____
16.	$7\frac{9}{2}$ _____	$\frac{12}{7}$ _____	$2\frac{9}{8}$ _____

Check What You Know

Adding Fractions

Add. Write answers in simplest form.

	a	b	c	d
1.	$\dfrac{1}{8}$ $+\dfrac{6}{8}$	$\dfrac{3}{7}$ $+\dfrac{3}{7}$	$\dfrac{2}{6}$ $+\dfrac{1}{6}$	$\dfrac{4}{9}$ $+\dfrac{3}{9}$
2.	$\dfrac{7}{8}$ $+\dfrac{7}{8}$	$\dfrac{4}{5}$ $+\dfrac{2}{8}$	$\dfrac{8}{10}$ $+\dfrac{7}{10}$	$\dfrac{3}{6}$ $+\dfrac{2}{4}$
3.	$1\dfrac{5}{8}$ $+6\dfrac{1}{8}$	$4\dfrac{2}{3}$ $+7\dfrac{2}{9}$	$3\dfrac{1}{3}$ $+9\dfrac{1}{2}$	$8\dfrac{7}{9}$ $+8\dfrac{8}{9}$

Find the equivalent fraction.

4. $\dfrac{4}{7} = \dfrac{}{14}$ $\dfrac{1}{9} = \dfrac{}{18}$ $\dfrac{5}{6} = \dfrac{}{12}$ $\dfrac{5}{12} = \dfrac{}{60}$

5. $\dfrac{2}{5} = \dfrac{}{20}$ $7 = \dfrac{}{6}$ $6 = \dfrac{}{11}$ $4 = \dfrac{}{7}$

Check What You Know

Adding Fractions

SHOW YOUR WORK

Solve each problem. Write answers in simplest form.

6. Mrs. Thompson's cookie recipe includes $\frac{1}{3}$ cup sugar and 4 cups flour. How many cups of sugar and flour does Mrs. Thompson need for her cookies?

Mrs. Thompson needs _____ cups of ingredients.

6.

7. Mr. Chen is going to the post office with two packages. One package weighs $6\frac{3}{8}$ kilograms and the other weighs $2\frac{1}{8}$ kilograms. How many kilograms are the two packages combined?

The packages weigh _____ kilograms combined.

7.

8. Carrie is running in a track meet. In one race, she must run $\frac{1}{4}$ mile and in a second race, she must run $1\frac{2}{5}$ miles. How many miles must Carrie run in all?

Carrie must run _____ miles.

8.

9. Mr. Cabezas is buying paint. He bought $4\frac{2}{7}$ gallons of blue paint and $3\frac{1}{2}$ gallons of purple paint. How many gallons of blue and purple paint did Mr. Cabezas buy?

Mr. Cabezas bought _____ gallons of paint.

9. | **10.**

10. Mrs. Lieu has cooked $3\frac{1}{8}$ pounds of potatoes. There are $\frac{2}{3}$ more to be cooked. How many pounds of potatoes are there in all?

There are _____ pounds of potatoes.

Lesson 5.1 Adding Fractions with Like Denominators

Add the numerators.
Use the common denominator.

$$\frac{1}{5} + \frac{2}{5} = \frac{1+2}{5}$$

Denominators are called **like** or **common** when they share the same number.

Add the numerators.

Use the common denominator.

$$\begin{array}{r} \frac{1}{5} \\ +\frac{2}{5} \\ \hline \frac{3}{5} \end{array}$$

Add. Write answers in simplest form.

	a	b	c	d	e
1.	$\frac{1}{3}$ $+\frac{1}{3}$	$\frac{2}{5}$ $+\frac{1}{5}$	$\frac{2}{9}$ $+\frac{5}{9}$	$\frac{5}{7}$ $+\frac{1}{7}$	$\frac{1}{6}$ $+\frac{1}{6}$
2.	$\frac{2}{5}$ $+\frac{2}{5}$	$\frac{2}{7}$ $+\frac{2}{7}$	$\frac{5}{8}$ $+\frac{1}{8}$	$\frac{1}{10}$ $+\frac{3}{10}$	$\frac{1}{5}$ $+\frac{3}{5}$
3.	$\frac{3}{8}$ $+\frac{1}{8}$	$\frac{5}{9}$ $+\frac{1}{9}$	$\frac{7}{11}$ $+\frac{2}{11}$	$\frac{4}{7}$ $+\frac{1}{7}$	$\frac{1}{12}$ $+\frac{5}{12}$
4.	$\frac{1}{4}$ $+\frac{2}{4}$	$\frac{3}{10}$ $+\frac{3}{10}$	$\frac{1}{5}$ $+\frac{3}{5}$	$\frac{3}{11}$ $+\frac{5}{11}$	$\frac{2}{7}$ $+\frac{4}{7}$

Lesson 5.1 Adding Fractions with Like Denominators

Add.

$$\frac{5}{9}$$
$$+\frac{8}{9}$$
$$\frac{13}{9} = 1\frac{4}{9}$$

Change the improper fraction to a mixed numeral and simplify.

To change the improper fraction $\frac{13}{9}$ to a mixed numeral: $13 \div 9 = 1 \text{ r } 4$.

$\frac{13}{9} = 1$ one and $\frac{4}{9}$ of one

$= 1\frac{4}{9}$

Add. Write answers in simplest form.

	a	b	c	d	e
1.	$\frac{3}{4}$ $+\frac{3}{4}$	$\frac{1}{2}$ $+\frac{1}{2}$	$\frac{4}{5}$ $+\frac{4}{5}$	$\frac{2}{6}$ $+\frac{5}{6}$	$\frac{3}{7}$ $+\frac{6}{7}$
2.	$\frac{3}{5}$ $+\frac{4}{5}$	$\frac{1}{3}$ $+\frac{2}{3}$	$\frac{2}{7}$ $+\frac{5}{7}$	$\frac{5}{8}$ $+\frac{5}{8}$	$\frac{2}{4}$ $+\frac{3}{4}$
3.	$\frac{7}{10}$ $+\frac{9}{10}$	$\frac{4}{7}$ $+\frac{5}{7}$	$\frac{7}{8}$ $+\frac{7}{8}$	$\frac{2}{5}$ $+\frac{3}{5}$	$\frac{7}{9}$ $+\frac{5}{9}$
4.	$\frac{7}{8}$ $+\frac{3}{8}$	$\frac{7}{11}$ $+\frac{6}{11}$	$\frac{8}{9}$ $+\frac{7}{9}$	$\frac{4}{7}$ $+\frac{3}{7}$	$\frac{11}{12}$ $+\frac{7}{12}$

Lesson 5.2 Adding Mixed Numerals with Like Denominators

$3\dfrac{4}{9}$	Add the fractions.	$\dfrac{4}{9} + \dfrac{2}{9} = \dfrac{6}{9}$
$+2\dfrac{2}{9}$	Add the whole numbers.	$3 + 2 = 5$
$5\dfrac{6}{9} = 5\dfrac{2}{3}$	Reduce to simplest form.	$\dfrac{6 \div 3}{9 \div 3} = \dfrac{2}{3}$

Add. Write answers in simplest form.

	a	b	c	d	e
1.	$3\dfrac{4}{7}$ $+5\dfrac{3}{7}$	$6\dfrac{4}{9}$ $+8\dfrac{5}{9}$	$7\dfrac{1}{6}$ $+3\dfrac{1}{6}$	$2\dfrac{2}{5}$ $+4\dfrac{4}{5}$	$3\dfrac{2}{11}$ $+8\dfrac{8}{11}$
2.	$9\dfrac{3}{10}$ $+2\dfrac{9}{10}$	$5\dfrac{1}{8}$ $+4\dfrac{3}{8}$	$1\dfrac{6}{7}$ $+3\dfrac{2}{7}$	$8\dfrac{3}{4}$ $+6\dfrac{3}{4}$	$2\dfrac{2}{9}$ $+7\dfrac{2}{9}$
3.	$6\dfrac{4}{11}$ $+1\dfrac{3}{11}$	$3\dfrac{1}{10}$ $+4\dfrac{9}{10}$	$6\dfrac{5}{6}$ $+5\dfrac{5}{6}$	$5\dfrac{3}{8}$ $+8\dfrac{3}{8}$	$1\dfrac{5}{7}$ $+6\dfrac{4}{7}$
4.	$2\dfrac{11}{12}$ $+7\dfrac{11}{12}$	$8\dfrac{3}{5}$ $+8\dfrac{1}{5}$	$9\dfrac{5}{12}$ $+4\dfrac{7}{12}$	$2\dfrac{8}{9}$ $+5\dfrac{7}{9}$	$7\dfrac{9}{10}$ $+6\dfrac{9}{10}$

Lesson 5.3 Problem Solving

SHOW YOUR WORK

Solve each problem. Write answers in simplest form.

1. Tom spends $\frac{4}{9}$ of his day working and $\frac{2}{9}$ of his day sleeping. How much of each day does Tom spend working and sleeping?

   Tom spends _____ of each day working and sleeping.

2. In parking lot A, $\frac{3}{5}$ of the cars are red. In parking lot B, $\frac{4}{5}$ of the cars are red. What fraction of all the cars are red?

   Of all the cars, _____ are red.

3. Last week, it rained two days in Ferndale. On the first day, there were $\frac{3}{4}$ of an inch of rain. On the second day, there were 2 inches of rain. How many inches of rain fell last week in Ferndale?

   _____ inches of rain fell last week.

4. It takes Carlos $2\frac{1}{6}$ days to make a model airplane and $1\frac{5}{6}$ days to make a model car. How many days will it take Carlos to make both?

   It will take _____ days for Carlos to make both.

5. As Howard is driving on the freeway, he sees a sign for Shoup Road $\frac{3}{4}$ mile away. Woodlake Avenue is $1\frac{1}{4}$ miles past Shoup. How far is Howard from Woodlake Avenue?

   Howard is _____ miles from Woodlake Avenue.

6. Michele is going to make lemonade. She will need $\frac{1}{3}$ cup sugar and $2\frac{2}{3}$ cups of water. How many total cups of sugar and water does Michele need?

   She needs _____ total cups.

1.	2.
3.	**4.**
5.	**6.**

Lesson 5.4 Finding Equivalent Fractions

Equivalent fractions name the same amount. To find equivalent fractions, multiply the numerator and denominator by the same nonzero number.

$$\frac{3}{5} = \frac{\square}{10}$$

$$\frac{3}{5} = \frac{3 \times 2}{5 \times 2}$$

$$\frac{3}{5} = \frac{6}{10}$$

$\frac{3}{5}$ and $\frac{6}{10}$ are equivalent fractions.

$$\frac{3}{5} = \frac{\square}{20}$$

$$\frac{3}{5} = \frac{3 \times 4}{5 \times 4}$$

$$\frac{3}{5} = \frac{12}{20}$$

$\frac{3}{5}$ and $\frac{12}{20}$ are equivalent fractions.

Find the equivalent fraction.

	a	b	c
1.	$\frac{2}{5} = \frac{}{15}$	$\frac{3}{4} = \frac{}{20}$	$\frac{1}{2} = \frac{}{8}$
2.	$\frac{1}{3} = \frac{}{12}$	$\frac{4}{7} = \frac{}{14}$	$\frac{3}{5} = \frac{}{35}$
3.	$\frac{6}{7} = \frac{}{21}$	$\frac{5}{6} = \frac{}{18}$	$\frac{2}{3} = \frac{}{18}$
4.	$\frac{7}{8} = \frac{}{24}$	$\frac{4}{5} = \frac{}{10}$	$\frac{5}{7} = \frac{}{28}$

Lesson 5.4 Finding Equivalent Fractions

$8 = \dfrac{\square}{4}$

$8 = \dfrac{8}{1}$ Rewrite the whole number as a fraction whose denominator is one.

$\dfrac{8 \times 4}{1 \times 4} = \dfrac{32}{4}$ Multiply the numerator and denominator by the same number.

$8 = \dfrac{32}{4}$ $\dfrac{8}{1}$ and $\dfrac{32}{4}$ are equivalent fractions.

Find the equivalent fraction.

	a	b	c
1.	$\dfrac{1}{3} = \dfrac{}{6}$	$\dfrac{3}{5} = \dfrac{}{15}$	$\dfrac{2}{9} = \dfrac{}{27}$
2.	$\dfrac{6}{7} = \dfrac{}{14}$	$2 = \dfrac{}{3}$	$5 = \dfrac{}{7}$
3.	$7 = \dfrac{}{5}$	$\dfrac{5}{8} = \dfrac{}{32}$	$1 = \dfrac{}{6}$
4.	$3 = \dfrac{}{9}$	$\dfrac{8}{11} = \dfrac{}{33}$	$\dfrac{5}{6} = \dfrac{}{30}$
5.	$6 = \dfrac{}{3}$	$\dfrac{7}{9} = \dfrac{}{18}$	$8 = \dfrac{}{6}$

Lesson 5.5   Adding Fractions with Unlike Denominators

$$\begin{aligned} \frac{1}{7} \times \frac{3}{3} &= \frac{3}{21} \\ +\frac{2}{3} \times \frac{7}{7} &= +\frac{14}{21} \\ &\quad\ \ \frac{17}{21} \end{aligned}$$

To add fractions, the denominators must be the same. When you have unlike denominators, find the **least common multiple (LCM)** and rename the fractions.

In the example, the denominators are 3 and 7, so find the LCM of 3 and 7.

Multiples of 3: 3, 6, 9, 12, 15, 18, ⑳, 24

Multiples of 7: 7, 14, ㉑, 28

$$\begin{aligned} \frac{6}{7} \times \frac{3}{3} &= \frac{18}{21} \\ +\frac{2}{3} \times \frac{7}{7} &= +\frac{14}{21} \\ &\quad\ \ \frac{32}{21} = 1\frac{11}{21} \end{aligned}$$

The least common multiple of 3 and 7 is 21. To change each fraction so it has the same denominator, multiply both the numerator and denominator by the same number.

If necessary, change improper fractions to mixed numerals in simplest form.

Add each fraction. Write answers in simplest form.

	a	b	c	d	e
1.	$\frac{3}{5}$ $+\frac{1}{4}$	$\frac{2}{3}$ $+\frac{2}{7}$	$\frac{1}{5}$ $+\frac{1}{7}$	$\frac{3}{8}$ $+\frac{1}{6}$	$\frac{1}{2}$ $+\frac{1}{3}$
2.	$\frac{2}{9}$ $+\frac{5}{8}$	$\frac{6}{7}$ $+\frac{1}{3}$	$\frac{2}{5}$ $+\frac{5}{7}$	$\frac{7}{10}$ $+\frac{1}{3}$	$\frac{3}{7}$ $+\frac{1}{8}$
3.	$\frac{2}{3}$ $+\frac{1}{5}$	$\frac{4}{7}$ $+\frac{5}{9}$	$\frac{3}{4}$ $+\frac{3}{10}$	$\frac{7}{8}$ $+\frac{2}{5}$	$\frac{8}{9}$ $+\frac{6}{7}$

Lesson 5.5 Adding Fractions with Unlike Denominators

$$\begin{aligned}\frac{3}{5} \times \frac{2}{2} &= \frac{6}{10}\\ +\frac{1}{10} \times \frac{1}{1} &= +\frac{1}{10}\\ &\quad\;\; \frac{7}{10}\end{aligned}$$

The denominators are 5 and 10. Since $2 \times 5 = 10$, only rename $\frac{3}{5}$ to $\frac{6}{10}$. Then, add the fractions.

When necessary, change improper fractions to mixed numerals in simplest form.

$$\begin{aligned}\frac{3}{5} \times \frac{2}{2} &= \frac{6}{10}\\ +\frac{9}{10} \times \frac{1}{1} &= +\frac{9}{10}\\ &\quad\;\; \frac{15}{10} = 1\frac{5}{10} = 1\frac{1}{2}\end{aligned}$$

Add each fraction. Write answers in simplest form.

	a	b	c	d	e
1.	$\dfrac{1}{2}$ $+\dfrac{3}{4}$	$\dfrac{3}{5}$ $+\dfrac{1}{10}$	$\dfrac{5}{6}$ $+\dfrac{3}{4}$	$\dfrac{1}{3}$ $+\dfrac{5}{6}$	$\dfrac{2}{3}$ $+\dfrac{1}{12}$
2.	$\dfrac{3}{8}$ $+\dfrac{1}{4}$	$\dfrac{2}{3}$ $+\dfrac{5}{9}$	$\dfrac{5}{12}$ $+\dfrac{7}{8}$	$\dfrac{1}{2}$ $+\dfrac{7}{10}$	$\dfrac{3}{4}$ $+\dfrac{5}{6}$
3.	$\dfrac{5}{7}$ $+\dfrac{4}{14}$	$\dfrac{1}{6}$ $+\dfrac{7}{8}$	$\dfrac{9}{10}$ $+\dfrac{5}{8}$	$\dfrac{2}{9}$ $+\dfrac{11}{12}$	$\dfrac{5}{6}$ $+\dfrac{8}{9}$

Lesson 5.6 Adding Mixed Numerals with Unlike Denominators

$$3\frac{5}{8} \times 1 = 3\frac{5}{8}$$

Find the common denominator (8) and rename the fractions.

$$+2\frac{1}{2} \times 4 = +2\frac{4}{8}$$

Add the fractions.

$$5\frac{9}{8} = 6\frac{1}{8}$$

Add the whole numbers.

Add the mixed numerals. Write answers in simplest form.

	a	b	c	d
1.	$2\frac{1}{2}$ $+3\frac{2}{5}$	$1\frac{2}{3}$ $+6\frac{1}{5}$	$4\frac{2}{7}$ $+3\frac{3}{4}$	$5\frac{1}{4}$ $+2\frac{1}{5}$
2.	$8\frac{1}{6}$ $+1\frac{4}{7}$	$2\frac{5}{6}$ $+6\frac{3}{5}$	$7\frac{3}{8}$ $+3\frac{1}{3}$	$4\frac{2}{9}$ $+9\frac{1}{2}$
3.	$9\frac{5}{6}$ $+6\frac{5}{8}$	$4\frac{1}{7}$ $+10\frac{2}{3}$	$8\frac{1}{9}$ $+2\frac{6}{7}$	$7\frac{3}{10}$ $+1\frac{5}{6}$
4.	$5\frac{7}{10}$ $+8\frac{2}{3}$	$11\frac{4}{5}$ $+2\frac{8}{9}$	$6\frac{7}{8}$ $+5\frac{1}{6}$	$9\frac{5}{7}$ $+9\frac{9}{10}$

Lesson 5.7   Problem Solving

Solve each problem. Write answers in simplest form.

1. Caroline needs $3\frac{1}{7}$ cups of sugar for her first batch of brownies and $2\frac{8}{9}$ cups of sugar for a second batch. How much sugar does she need in all?

   Caroline needs _____ cups of sugar.

2. Robert's gas tank has $5\frac{3}{5}$ gallons of gas in it. If he adds $7\frac{2}{3}$ gallons, how much gas will be in the tank?

   There will be _____ gallons of gas in the tank.

3. A hamburger weighs $\frac{1}{3}$ pound, and an order of french fries weighs $\frac{1}{4}$ pound. How many pounds total will a meal of hamburger and french fries weigh?

   The meal will weigh _____ pound.

4. John is $5\frac{1}{4}$ feet tall and Jamar is $\frac{5}{8}$ foot taller than John. How tall is Jamar?

   Jamar is _____ feet tall.

5. Mrs. Stevenson has used $4\frac{2}{3}$ inches of string. She needs $1\frac{6}{7}$ inches more. How much string will Mrs. Stevenson have used when she is done?

   Mrs. Stevenson will have used _____ inches of string.

6. It takes Lacy $8\frac{1}{3}$ seconds to climb up the slide and $2\frac{1}{4}$ seconds to go down the slide. How many seconds is Lacy's trip up and down the slide?

   Lacy's trip is _____ seconds long.

1.	2.
3.	4.
5.	6.

Check What You Learned

Adding Fractions

Add. Write answers in simplest form.

	a	b	c	d
1.	$\dfrac{4}{6}$ $+\dfrac{1}{6}$	$\dfrac{3}{7}$ $+\dfrac{2}{7}$	$\dfrac{2}{9}$ $+\dfrac{6}{9}$	$\dfrac{7}{8}$ $+\dfrac{2}{8}$
2.	$\dfrac{5}{11}$ $\dfrac{9}{11}$ $+\phantom{\dfrac{}{}}$	$\dfrac{8}{9}$ $+\dfrac{8}{9}$	$\dfrac{7}{12}$ $+\dfrac{3}{5}$	$\dfrac{2}{5}$ $+\dfrac{9}{10}$
3.	$\dfrac{5}{8}$ $+\dfrac{5}{6}$	$\dfrac{2}{7}$ $+\dfrac{8}{10}$	$5\dfrac{2}{5}$ $+7\dfrac{3}{5}$	$8\dfrac{3}{10}$ $+9\dfrac{2}{4}$

Find the equivalent fraction.

4. $\dfrac{7}{12} = \dfrac{}{60}$ $\dfrac{8}{9} = \dfrac{}{81}$ $4 = \dfrac{}{8}$ $\dfrac{7}{10} = \dfrac{}{30}$

5. $7 = \dfrac{}{7}$ $\dfrac{5}{11} = \dfrac{}{33}$ $3 = \dfrac{}{6}$ $9 = \dfrac{}{4}$

Check What You Learned

Adding Fractions

Solve each problem. Write answers in simplest form.

6. Susanne is baking a birthday cake. She has $1\frac{2}{5}$ cups of sugar and $\frac{3}{5}$ cup of flour. How much sugar and flour does Susanne have?

   Susanne has _____ cups of sugar and flour.

7. Mrs. Heron wants to plant a garden in her front and back yard. She needs 3 bags of fertilizer for the front and $4\frac{1}{6}$ bags of fertilizer for the back. How many bags of fertilizer does Mrs. Heron need in all?

   Mrs. Heron needs _____ bags of fertilizer.

8. The Greenline Express train takes $3\frac{2}{9}$ days to go from Greensville to Uniondale and $2\frac{3}{5}$ days to go from Uniondale to Ford Hall. How many days will it take the Greenline Express to go from Greensville to Ford Hall?

   It will take the train _____ days to make the trip.

9. Larry worked $7\frac{3}{5}$ hours on Monday and $6\frac{1}{6}$ hours on Wednesday. How many hours did Larry work during the two days?

   Larry worked _____ hours during the two days.

10. On Saturday, Anthony watched $5\frac{1}{3}$ hours of television. On Sunday, he watched $3\frac{5}{6}$ hours of television. How many hours of television did Anthony watch throughout the weekend?

    Anthony watched _____ hours of television.

6.	7.
8.	9.
10.	

Check What You Know

Subtracting Fractions

Subtract. Write answers in simplest form.

	a	b	c	d
1.	$\dfrac{7}{8}$ $-\dfrac{1}{8}$	$\dfrac{5}{9}$ $-\dfrac{4}{9}$	$\dfrac{8}{10}$ $-\dfrac{3}{10}$	$\dfrac{7}{12}$ $-\dfrac{1}{12}$
2.	$\dfrac{7}{8}$ $-\dfrac{3}{4}$	$\dfrac{6}{7}$ $-\dfrac{4}{5}$	$\dfrac{4}{7}$ $-\dfrac{2}{9}$	6 $-\dfrac{2}{3}$
3.	2 $-\dfrac{1}{5}$	9 $-\dfrac{9}{10}$	1 $-\dfrac{7}{8}$	$4\dfrac{5}{6}$ $-1\dfrac{3}{6}$
4.	$8\dfrac{9}{10}$ $-4\dfrac{3}{10}$	$7\dfrac{3}{7}$ $-5\dfrac{2}{7}$	$6\dfrac{1}{4}$ $-2\dfrac{1}{6}$	$9\dfrac{7}{9}$ $-5\dfrac{1}{2}$

NAME Victoria Kwei

Check What You Know

SHOW YOUR WORK

Subtracting Fractions

Solve each problem. Write answers in simplest form.

5. Julianne needs 7 yards of string for her kite. She has $\frac{5}{8}$ yard. How many more yards does Julianne need for her kite?

   Julianne needs ___$6\frac{3}{8}$___ more yards of string.

6. Enzo's Pizzeria makes a large pizza with $\frac{7}{9}$ ounce of pepperoni and $\frac{4}{9}$ ounce of pineapple. How much more pepperoni than pineapple does a large pizza have?

   There is ___$\frac{1}{3}$___ ounce more of pepperoni.

7. Marlon watched a movie $1\frac{8}{9}$ hours long. Jessie watched a movie $2\frac{2}{7}$ hours long. How much longer was Jessie's movie than Marlon's?

   Jessie's movie was ___$\frac{25}{63}$___ hour longer.

8. David practiced soccer twice last week. On Monday, he practiced $2\frac{1}{3}$ hours. On Wednesday, he practiced $1\frac{7}{9}$ hours. How much longer did David practice on Monday?

   David practiced ___$\frac{5}{9}$___ hour longer on Monday.

9. The Thompsons are $3\frac{1}{2}$ miles from Liberty Canyon Drive and $2\frac{3}{4}$ miles from Lost Hills Road. How much further is Liberty Canyon Drive from the Thompsons' than Lost Hills Road?

   It is ___$\frac{3}{4}$___ mile further from the Thompsons' than Lost Hills Road.

5.

$$7$$
$$-\frac{5}{8}$$
$$\overline{6\frac{3}{8}}$$

6.

$$\frac{7}{9}$$
$$-\frac{4}{9}$$
$$\overline{\frac{1}{3}}$$

7.

$$2\frac{2}{7}$$
$$-1\frac{8}{9}$$
$$\overline{\frac{25}{63}}$$

8.

$$2\frac{1}{3}$$
$$-1\frac{7}{9}$$
$$\overline{\frac{5}{9}}$$

9.

$$3\frac{1}{2}$$
$$-2\frac{3}{4}$$
$$\overline{\frac{3}{4}}$$

Lesson 6.1 Subtracting Fractions with Like Denominators

Subtract the numerators.

$$\frac{7}{10} - \frac{3}{10} = \frac{7-3}{10} = \frac{4}{10} = \frac{2}{5}$$

Use the common denominator.

Two denominators are called **like** or **common** when they share the same number.

$$\begin{array}{r} \frac{7}{10} \\ -\frac{3}{10} \\ \hline \frac{4}{10} = \frac{2}{5} \end{array}$$ Write in simplest form.

Subtract. Write answers in simplest form.

	a	b	c	d
1.	$\frac{5}{7}$ $-\frac{3}{7}$	$\frac{3}{4}$ $-\frac{1}{4}$	$\frac{7}{8}$ $-\frac{3}{8}$	$\frac{4}{5}$ $-\frac{2}{5}$
2.	$\frac{7}{9}$ $-\frac{1}{9}$	$\frac{5}{6}$ $-\frac{1}{6}$	$\frac{2}{9}$ $-\frac{1}{9}$	$\frac{6}{7}$ $-\frac{1}{7}$
3.	$\frac{4}{5}$ $-\frac{1}{5}$	$\frac{8}{10}$ $-\frac{3}{10}$	$\frac{7}{12}$ $-\frac{5}{12}$	$\frac{7}{8}$ $-\frac{5}{8}$
4.	$\frac{9}{10}$ $-\frac{7}{10}$	$\frac{3}{5}$ $-\frac{2}{5}$	$\frac{8}{9}$ $-\frac{5}{9}$	$\frac{8}{11}$ $-\frac{4}{11}$

Lesson 6.2 Subtracting Fractions from Whole Numbers

$$6 = 5\frac{3}{3}$$
$$-\frac{2}{3} = -\frac{2}{3}$$
$$\overline{} \quad 5\frac{1}{3}$$

Rename the whole number as a mixed numeral so that the denominator is the same as that of the fraction.

$$6 = 5 + 1$$
$$= 5 + \frac{3}{3}$$
$$= 5\frac{3}{3}$$

Subtract. Write answers in simplest form.

	a	b	c	d	e

1.

a) $4 - \frac{2}{3}$

b) $6 - \frac{1}{5}$

c) $1 - \frac{2}{7}$

d) $8 - \frac{1}{2}$

e) $4 - \frac{5}{6}$

2.

a) $7 - \frac{1}{6}$

b) $8 - \frac{1}{3}$

c) $2 - \frac{3}{8}$

d) $5 - \frac{5}{7}$

e) $9 - \frac{2}{5}$

3.

a) $5 - \frac{7}{10}$

b) $6 - \frac{3}{4}$

c) $3 - \frac{4}{11}$

d) $7 - \frac{5}{8}$

e) $8 - \frac{1}{4}$

Lesson 6.3 Subtracting Mixed Numerals with Like Denominators

$3\dfrac{2}{8} = \quad 2\dfrac{10}{8}$ $\quad \dfrac{2}{8}$ is less than $\dfrac{3}{8}$. Rename $3\dfrac{2}{8}$.

$-1\dfrac{3}{8} = -1\dfrac{3}{8}$ Subtract the fractions.

$\rule{1.5cm}{0.4pt} \quad \rule{1.5cm}{0.4pt}$

$\qquad\qquad 1\dfrac{7}{8}$ Subtract the whole numbers.

$3 = 2 + 1 + \dfrac{2}{8}$

$= 2 + \dfrac{8}{8} + \dfrac{2}{8} = 2\dfrac{10}{8}$

Subtract. Write answers in simplest form.

	a	b	c	d	e

1.
  a. $3\dfrac{3}{4}$ $-1\dfrac{1}{4}$
  b. $6\dfrac{2}{7}$ $-2\dfrac{1}{7}$
  c. $9\dfrac{7}{8}$ $-3\dfrac{5}{8}$
  d. $8\dfrac{5}{6}$ $-4\dfrac{1}{6}$
  e. $6\dfrac{5}{8}$ $-3\dfrac{3}{8}$

2.
  a. $7\dfrac{7}{9}$ $-4\dfrac{4}{9}$
  b. $5\dfrac{7}{10}$ $-3\dfrac{1}{10}$
  c. $6\dfrac{3}{5}$ $-4\dfrac{2}{5}$
  d. $9\dfrac{3}{7}$ $-7\dfrac{3}{7}$
  e. $8\dfrac{7}{9}$ $-7\dfrac{2}{9}$

3.
  a. $6\dfrac{3}{5}$ $-5\dfrac{1}{5}$
  b. $4\dfrac{5}{7}$ $-1\dfrac{2}{7}$
  c. $7\dfrac{9}{10}$ $-2\dfrac{3}{10}$
  d. $8\dfrac{11}{12}$ $-1\dfrac{7}{12}$
  e. $6\dfrac{8}{9}$ $-3\dfrac{7}{9}$

Lesson 6.4 Problem Solving

SHOW YOUR WORK

Solve each problem. Write answers in simplest form.

1. Becky is making a salad with tomatoes and olives on top. If Becky uses $\frac{5}{7}$ cup of tomatoes and $\frac{2}{7}$ cup of olives, how many more tomatoes will Becky use than olives?

   Becky will use ____$\frac{3}{7}$____ cup more of tomatoes than olives.

2. Joe had 2 pints of ice cream. He ate $\frac{3}{5}$ pint of the ice cream. How much ice cream remains?

   ____$1\frac{2}{5}$____ pints of ice cream remain.

3. The beach is $6\frac{9}{10}$ miles from the Cabrera family. They have driven $2\frac{3}{10}$ miles toward the beach. How many more miles must the Cabrera family drive?

   The Cabrera family must drive ____$4\frac{3}{5}$____ more miles.

4. Jaleela wants to paint her bedroom blue and gold. She has $4\frac{1}{8}$ gallons of blue paint and $2\frac{3}{8}$ gallons of gold paint. How much more blue paint does Jaleela have than gold paint?

   Jaleela has ____$1\frac{3}{4}$____ more gallons of blue paint than gold paint.

5. Travis is $5\frac{7}{12}$ feet tall. Nathan is $5\frac{11}{12}$ feet tall. How much taller is Nathan than Travis?

   Nathan is ____$\frac{1}{3}$____ foot taller than Travis.

6. Antonio must swim $9\frac{4}{5}$ meters to finish the race. He has swum $4\frac{2}{5}$ meters. How many more meters must Antonio swim to finish?

   Antonio must swim ____$5\frac{2}{5}$____ more meters.

1.	2.
$\frac{5}{7}$ $-\frac{2}{7}$ $\frac{3}{7}$	2 $-\frac{3}{5}$ $1\frac{2}{5}$
3.	**4.**
$6\frac{9}{10}$ $-2\frac{3}{10}$ $4\frac{3}{5}$	$4\frac{1}{8}$ $-2\frac{3}{8}$ $1\frac{3}{4}$
5.	**6.**
$5\frac{11}{12}$ $-5\frac{7}{12}$ $\frac{1}{3}$	$9\frac{4}{5}$ $-4\frac{2}{5}$ $5\frac{2}{5}$

Lesson 6.5 Subtracting Fractions with Unlike Denominators

$$\begin{array}{r} \dfrac{2 \times 7 =}{3 \times 7 =} \quad \dfrac{14}{21} \\[6pt] -\dfrac{2 \times 3 =}{7 \times 3 =} \quad -\dfrac{6}{21} \\[6pt] \dfrac{8}{21} \end{array}$$

When subtracting fractions that have different denominators, rename fractions to have a common denominator. Then, subtract fractions, and write the remainder in simplest form.

$$\begin{array}{r} \dfrac{5 \times 1 =}{6 \times 1 =} \quad \dfrac{5}{6} \\[6pt] -\dfrac{2 \times 2 =}{3 \times 2 =} \quad -\dfrac{4}{6} \\[6pt] \dfrac{1}{6} \end{array}$$

Subtract. Write answers in simplest form.

	a	b	c	d	e
1.	$\dfrac{3}{4}$ $-\dfrac{1}{2}$	$\dfrac{5}{6}$ $-\dfrac{1}{3}$	$\dfrac{9}{10}$ $-\dfrac{2}{5}$	$\dfrac{4}{7}$ $-\dfrac{1}{8}$	$\dfrac{5}{9}$ $-\dfrac{1}{3}$
2.	$\dfrac{2}{5}$ $-\dfrac{1}{9}$	$\dfrac{3}{5}$ $-\dfrac{2}{7}$	$\dfrac{2}{3}$ $-\dfrac{3}{8}$	$\dfrac{5}{6}$ $-\dfrac{1}{3}$	$\dfrac{3}{4}$ $-\dfrac{2}{9}$
3.	$\dfrac{7}{10}$ $-\dfrac{3}{6}$	$\dfrac{8}{9}$ $-\dfrac{1}{4}$	$\dfrac{7}{8}$ $-\dfrac{5}{12}$	$\dfrac{7}{10}$ $-\dfrac{1}{4}$	$\dfrac{4}{5}$ $-\dfrac{3}{7}$

Lesson 6.6 Subtracting Mixed Numerals with Unlike Denominators

$$6\frac{5}{7} \times \frac{3}{3} = 6\frac{15}{21}$$

Rename fractions to have common denominators.

$$-5\frac{1}{3} \times \frac{7}{7} = -5\frac{7}{21}$$

Subtract the fractions, then subtract the whole numbers.

$$1\frac{8}{21}$$

Write the remainder in simplest form.

Subtract. Write answers in simplest form.

	a	b	c	d	e
1.	$4\frac{2}{3}$ $-2\frac{1}{6}$	$7\frac{7}{8}$ $-2\frac{3}{4}$	$8\frac{9}{10}$ $-6\frac{2}{5}$	$8\frac{3}{4}$ $-4\frac{3}{8}$	$3\frac{1}{3}$ $-2\frac{2}{9}$
2.	$6\frac{5}{8}$ $-4\frac{3}{7}$	$5\frac{1}{2}$ $-1\frac{1}{6}$	$9\frac{7}{8}$ $-4\frac{2}{5}$	$9\frac{5}{9}$ $-3\frac{1}{3}$	$7\frac{7}{10}$ $-4\frac{4}{7}$
3.	$8\frac{8}{12}$ $-2\frac{3}{4}$	$9\frac{3}{10}$ $-6\frac{1}{8}$	$8\frac{4}{6}$ $-5\frac{2}{8}$	$6\frac{6}{7}$ $-3\frac{3}{5}$	$5\frac{5}{6}$ $-3\frac{1}{12}$
4.	$2\frac{1}{2}$ $-1\frac{4}{11}$	$5\frac{7}{10}$ $-2\frac{3}{8}$	$9\frac{7}{8}$ $-8\frac{2}{9}$	$7\frac{3}{4}$ $-6\frac{7}{12}$	$8\frac{9}{11}$ $-1\frac{3}{7}$

Lesson 6.7 Subtraction Practice

Subtract. Write answers in simplest form.

	a	b	c	d	e
1.	$\dfrac{5}{9}$ $-\dfrac{1}{9}$	$\dfrac{6}{7}$ $-\dfrac{3}{7}$	$\dfrac{9}{10}$ $-\dfrac{3}{5}$	$\dfrac{5}{6}$ $-\dfrac{2}{6}$	$\dfrac{6}{8}$ $-\dfrac{1}{2}$
2.	$\dfrac{11}{12}$ $-\dfrac{4}{6}$	$\dfrac{8}{9}$ $-\dfrac{3}{4}$	7 $-\dfrac{2}{9}$	$\dfrac{8}{9}$ $-\dfrac{2}{3}$	3 $-\dfrac{4}{7}$
3.	9 $-\dfrac{1}{10}$	$4\dfrac{3}{4}$ $-1\dfrac{1}{4}$	$8\dfrac{11}{12}$ $-3\dfrac{8}{12}$	1 $-\dfrac{7}{8}$	$6\dfrac{5}{6}$ $-1\dfrac{5}{6}$
4.	7 $-\dfrac{8}{11}$	$9\dfrac{6}{7}$ $-4\dfrac{2}{7}$	$3\dfrac{9}{10}$ $-2\dfrac{3}{10}$	$4\dfrac{7}{8}$ $-4\dfrac{2}{9}$	$9\dfrac{3}{4}$ $-1\dfrac{1}{2}$
5.	$4\dfrac{5}{6}$ $-2\dfrac{1}{6}$	$8\dfrac{3}{8}$ $-6\dfrac{1}{6}$	$7\dfrac{2}{3}$ $-6\dfrac{1}{4}$	$3\dfrac{1}{3}$ $-1\dfrac{3}{11}$	$6\dfrac{11}{12}$ $-4\dfrac{5}{6}$

Lesson 6.8   Problem Solving

Solve each problem. Write answers in simplest form.

1. Eric needs $\frac{1}{2}$ a deck of playing cards for a magic trick. He only has $\frac{2}{7}$ of a deck. What fraction of a deck does Eric need?

   Eric needs _____ $\frac{3}{14}$ _____ of a deck for his magic trick.

2. Randy ran $1\frac{3}{4}$ miles. Natasha ran $\frac{9}{10}$ mile. How many more miles did Randy run than Natasha?

   Randy ran _____ $\frac{17}{20}$ _____ mile more than Natasha.

3. A soccer ball when fully inflated weighs 6 ounces. Raymundo has inflated the ball to $4\frac{2}{3}$ ounces. How many more ounces must be added before the ball is fully inflated?

   The ball needs _____ $1\frac{1}{3}$ _____ more ounces to be fully inflated.

4. In January, employees at Home Real Estate Company worked $6\frac{3}{4}$ hours a day. In February, employees worked $7\frac{1}{8}$ hours a day. How many more hours did employees work daily during February than during January?

   Employees worked _____ $\frac{3}{8}$ _____ hour more during February.

5. Peter's hat size is $7\frac{3}{8}$ units. Cal's hat size is $6\frac{7}{12}$ units. How many units larger is Peter's hat size than Cal's?

   Peter's hat size is _____ $\frac{19}{24}$ _____ unit larger than Cal's.

6. Mrs. Anderson uses $3\frac{1}{5}$ cups of apples for her pies. Mrs. Woods uses $4\frac{2}{3}$ cups of apples for her pies. How many more cups of apples does Mrs. Woods use than Mrs. Anderson?

   Mrs. Woods uses _____ $1\frac{7}{15}$ _____ more cups of apples.

1.	2.
$\frac{1}{2}$ $-\frac{2}{7}$ $\overline{\frac{3}{14}}$	$1\frac{3}{4}$ $-\frac{9}{10}$ $\overline{\frac{17}{20}}$

3.	4.
6 $-4\frac{2}{3}$ $\overline{1\frac{1}{3}}$	$7\frac{1}{8}$ $-6\frac{3}{4}$ $\overline{\frac{3}{8}}$

5.	6.
$7\frac{3}{8}$ $-6\frac{7}{12}$ $\overline{\frac{19}{24}}$	$4\frac{2}{3}$ $-3\frac{1}{5}$ $\overline{1\frac{7}{15}}$

Check What You Learned

Subtracting Fractions

Subtract. Write answers in simplest form.

	a	b	c	d

1.

a) $\frac{5}{9} - \frac{2}{9}$

b) $\frac{6}{7} - \frac{5}{7}$

c) $\frac{3}{4} - \frac{1}{2}$

d) $\frac{5}{8} - \frac{1}{4}$

2.

a) $\frac{5}{6} - \frac{7}{12}$

b) $4 - \frac{5}{6}$

c) $7 - \frac{9}{10}$

d) $2 - \frac{1}{2}$

3.

a) $6\frac{2}{3} - 4\frac{1}{3}$

b) $9\frac{6}{7} - 5\frac{2}{7}$

c) $3\frac{11}{12} - 1\frac{7}{12}$

d) $\frac{5}{7} - \frac{1}{3}$

4.

a) $\frac{7}{8} - \frac{1}{9}$

b) $\frac{8}{11} - \frac{4}{9}$

c) $\frac{5}{6} - \frac{3}{8}$

d) $2\frac{5}{8} - \frac{1}{4}$

5.

a) $6\frac{5}{6} - 2\frac{8}{9}$

b) $8\frac{3}{5} - 6\frac{1}{3}$

c) $5\frac{2}{7} - 4\frac{1}{4}$

d) $9\frac{1}{9} - 1\frac{4}{5}$

Check What You Learned

SHOW YOUR WORK

Subtracting Fractions

Solve each problem. Write answers in simplest form.

6. Henry has $\frac{7}{8}$ hour to finish reading a book before class. After $\frac{3}{8}$ hour, he is almost done. How much more time does Henry have to finish reading his book?

   Henry has ___ $\frac{1}{2}$ ___ hour to finish reading his book.

7. Tad is allowed to use the computer for $\frac{1}{2}$ hour. He has been using the computer for $\frac{4}{9}$ hour. How much more time does Tad have on the computer?

   Tad has ___ $\frac{1}{18}$ ___ hour more on the computer.

8. Julian scored a basket at $8\frac{4}{9}$ feet from the basketball hoop. Adam scored a basket $12\frac{1}{2}$ feet from the hoop. How much farther was Adam's shot than Julian's shot?

   Adam's shot was ___ $4\frac{1}{18}$ ___ feet farther than Julian's.

9. The Ramirez family bought $3\frac{1}{2}$ gallons of orange juice. They drank $2\frac{3}{8}$ gallons. How many gallons of orange juice remain?

   The Ramirez family has ___ $1\frac{1}{8}$ ___ gallons of orange juice remaining.

10. Kara needs $3\frac{1}{2}$ feet of ribbon to make bows. She has $2\frac{7}{10}$ feet of ribbon. How much more ribbon does Kara need?

    Kara needs ___ $\frac{4}{5}$ ___ foot of ribbon.

6.	7.
$\frac{7}{8}$ $-\frac{3}{8}$ $\frac{1}{2}$	$\frac{1}{2}$ $-\frac{4}{9}$ $\frac{1}{18}$

8.	9.
$12\frac{1}{2}$ $-8\frac{4}{9}$ $4\frac{1}{18}$	$3\frac{1}{2}$ $-2\frac{3}{8}$ $1\frac{1}{8}$

10.
$3\frac{1}{2}$ $-2\frac{7}{10}$ $\frac{4}{5}$

Mid-Test Chapters 1–6

Add.

	a	b	c	d
1.	77 +51 128	42 +79 121	68 +95 163	326 + 14 340
2.	819 + 36 855	429 +228 657	3647 + 395 4,042	2918 +4312 7,230
3.	76455 + 3787 80,242	153916 + 43226 197,142	898792 +355638 1,254,430	217 349 +812 1,378
4.	4379 148 + 822 5,349	29274 3424 + 192 32,890	1763 2819 7224 +6318 18,124	42914 73699 72177 +51312 240,092

Subtract.

	a	b	c	d
5.	83 −64 19	32 −18 14	147 − 32 115	842 − 46 796
6.	376 − 88 288	749 −214 535	1736 − 498 1,238	3225 − 438 2,787
7.	2718 − 329 2,389	9190 − 364 8,826	42763 − 3949 38,814	60714 − 3847 56,867
8.	129142 − 39779 89,363	852414 − 93558 758,856	342197 −157098 185,099	829172 − 92485 736,687

Mid-Test   Chapters 1–6

Multiply.

	a	**b**	**c**	**d**
9.	$\begin{array}{r} 12 \\ \times\ 7 \\ \hline 84 \end{array}$	$\begin{array}{r} 24 \\ \times\ 9 \\ \hline 216 \end{array}$	$\begin{array}{r} 312 \\ \times\ 4 \\ \hline 1{,}248 \end{array}$	$\begin{array}{r} 3826 \\ \times\ 8 \\ \hline 30{,}608 \end{array}$
10.	$\begin{array}{r} 446 \\ \times\ 21 \\ \hline 9{,}366 \end{array}$	$\begin{array}{r} 376 \\ \times\ 18 \\ \hline 6{,}768 \end{array}$	$\begin{array}{r} 1824 \\ \times\ 16 \\ \hline 29{,}184 \end{array}$	$\begin{array}{r} 6829 \\ \times\ 27 \\ \hline 184{,}383 \end{array}$
11.	$\begin{array}{r} 163 \\ \times 241 \\ \hline 39{,}283 \end{array}$	$\begin{array}{r} 738 \\ \times 284 \\ \hline 209{,}592 \end{array}$	$\begin{array}{r} 6199 \\ \times\ 534 \\ \hline 3{,}310{,}266 \end{array}$	$\begin{array}{r} 7189 \\ \times\ 396 \\ \hline 2{,}846{,}844 \end{array}$

Divide.

12. $4\overline{)18}$ $4r2$	$8\overline{)27}$ $3r3$	$6\overline{)321}$ $53r3$	$9\overline{)472}$ $52r4$
13. $2\overline{)3216}$ $1{,}608$	$12\overline{)5178}$ $431r6$	$25\overline{)829}$ $33r4$	$53\overline{)3724}$ $70r14$
14. $31\overline{)734}$ $23r21$	$37\overline{)2558}$ $69r5$	$22\overline{)46376}$ $2{,}108$	$84\overline{)37219}$ $443r7$

CHAPTERS 1–6 MID-TEST

Mid-Test Chapters 1–6

Find the greatest common factor for each set of numbers.

	a	b	c
15.	27 and 72	32 and 36	6 and 51
	9	4	3
16.	18 and 21	19 and 76	63 and 99
	3	19	9

Write each improper fraction as a mixed numeral in simplest form.

17. $\frac{18}{8}$ $2\frac{1}{4}$ $\frac{51}{9}$ $5\frac{2}{3}$ $\frac{34}{3}$ $11\frac{1}{3}$

18. $\frac{53}{12}$ $4\frac{5}{12}$ $\frac{82}{8}$ $10\frac{1}{4}$ $\frac{66}{7}$ $9\frac{3}{7}$

Write each mixed numeral as an improper fraction.

19. $4\frac{1}{3}$ $\frac{13}{3}$ $7\frac{5}{9}$ $\frac{68}{9}$ $1\frac{7}{10}$ $\frac{17}{10}$

20. $3\frac{3}{4}$ $\frac{15}{4}$ $5\frac{11}{12}$ $\frac{71}{12}$ $8\frac{2}{9}$ $\frac{74}{9}$

Simplify each of the following.

21. $\frac{18}{20}$ $\frac{9}{10}$ $\frac{28}{35}$ $\frac{4}{5}$ $2\frac{2}{12}$ $2\frac{1}{6}$

22. $3\frac{4}{6}$ $3\frac{2}{3}$ $\frac{51}{6}$ $8\frac{1}{2}$ $7\frac{8}{12}$ $7\frac{2}{3}$

23. $4\frac{12}{5}$ $6\frac{2}{5}$ $6\frac{10}{4}$ $8\frac{1}{2}$ $9\frac{9}{4}$ $11\frac{1}{4}$

Mid-Test Chapters 1–6

Add or subtract the given fractions. Write answers in simplest form.

	a	b	c	d

24.

a. $\frac{3}{4} + \frac{1}{4} = 1$

b. $\frac{2}{7} + \frac{3}{5} = \frac{31}{35}$

c. $\frac{7}{8} + \frac{1}{3} = 1\frac{5}{24}$

d. $5 + \frac{2}{3} = 5\frac{2}{3}$

25.

a. $\frac{5}{8} - \frac{1}{8} = \frac{1}{2}$

b. $\frac{6}{9} - \frac{2}{3} = 0$

c. $\frac{10}{11} - \frac{4}{5} = \frac{6}{55}$

d. $7 - \frac{3}{4} = 6\frac{1}{4}$

26.

a. $2\frac{1}{3} + 4\frac{2}{3} = 7$

b. $6\frac{6}{7} + 7\frac{3}{7} = 14\frac{2}{7}$

c. $8\frac{1}{3} + 8\frac{5}{7} = 17\frac{1}{21}$

d. $2\frac{5}{8} + 9\frac{3}{4} = 12\frac{3}{8}$

27.

a. $9\frac{6}{8} - 4\frac{1}{8} = 5\frac{5}{8}$

b. $5\frac{7}{12} - 1\frac{5}{12} = 4\frac{1}{6}$

c. $7\frac{1}{4} - 3\frac{2}{9} = 4\frac{1}{36}$

d. $2\frac{5}{6} - 1\frac{1}{8} = 1\frac{17}{24}$

28.

a. $4\frac{1}{2} + 7\frac{3}{5} = 12\frac{1}{10}$

b. $2\frac{2}{7} + 8\frac{8}{3} = 12\frac{20}{21}$

c. $6\frac{9}{4} - 5\frac{3}{4} = 2\frac{1}{2}$

d. $6\frac{7}{3} - 2\frac{3}{2} = 4\frac{5}{6}$

Check What You Know

Multiplying Fractions

Multiply. Write answers in simplest form.

	a	b	c

1. $\dfrac{1}{2} \times \dfrac{1}{3} =$ _____ $\dfrac{3}{4} \times \dfrac{2}{7} =$ _____ $\dfrac{1}{4} \times \dfrac{4}{5} =$ _____

2. $\dfrac{2}{5} \times \dfrac{5}{8} =$ _____ $\dfrac{4}{9} \times \dfrac{1}{2} =$ _____ $5 \times \dfrac{2}{7} =$ _____

3. $3 \times \dfrac{4}{5} =$ _____ $\dfrac{6}{7} \times 7 =$ _____ $\dfrac{3}{4} \times 2 =$ _____

4. $8 \times 1\dfrac{3}{7} =$ _____ $4 \times 5\dfrac{1}{2} =$ _____ $2\dfrac{1}{7} \times 3 =$ _____

5. $7 \times 2\dfrac{1}{2} =$ _____ $3\dfrac{7}{10} \times 5 =$ _____ $2\dfrac{3}{4} \times 1\dfrac{2}{5} =$ _____

6. $3\dfrac{1}{9} \times 2\dfrac{1}{4} =$ _____ $4\dfrac{5}{12} \times 1\dfrac{1}{3} =$ _____ $2\dfrac{3}{4} \times 5\dfrac{1}{5} =$ _____

Check What You Know

NAME Victoria Kwei

Multiplying Fractions

SHOW YOUR WORK

Solve each problem. Write answers in simplest form.

7. Aimee lives $\frac{8}{9}$ mile from the park. She has walked $\frac{3}{5}$ of the way to the park. How far has Aimee walked?

Aimee has walked _____ $\frac{8}{15}$ _____ mile.

8. A single serving of jello requires $\frac{3}{8}$ cup sugar. How much sugar is needed for 6 servings?

_____ $2\frac{1}{4}$ _____ cups are needed.

9. Every day Sheila runs $\frac{4}{7}$ mile. If she runs for 9 days, how far will Sheila have run?

She will have run _____ $5\frac{1}{7}$ _____ miles.

10. Jason put down a tile floor in his basement. He placed 18 tiles across the floor. Each tile is $12\frac{5}{8}$ inches wide. How wide is the area he covered with tiles?

The area covered with tiles is _____ $139\frac{3}{4}$ _____ inches in width.

11. Ace driving school takes students on a course $9\frac{1}{7}$ miles long. If a student has completed $\frac{3}{4}$ of the course, how many miles has the student driven?

The student has driven _____ $6\frac{6}{7}$ _____ miles.

12. Suppose 8 books are stacked on top of one another. Each book is $1\frac{5}{9}$ inches thick. How high is the stack of books?

The stack of books is _____ $12\frac{4}{9}$ _____ inches high.

7.	8.
$\frac{8}{9}$ $\times \frac{3}{5}$ ————— $\frac{8}{15}$	$\frac{3}{8}$ $\times 6$ ————— $2\frac{1}{4}$

9.	10.
$\frac{4}{7}$ $\times 9$ ————— $5\frac{1}{7}$	$12\frac{5}{8}$ $\times 18$ ————— $139\frac{3}{4}$

11.	12.
$9\frac{1}{7}$ $\times \frac{3}{4}$ ————— $6\frac{6}{7}$	$1\frac{5}{9}$ $\times 8$ ————— $12\frac{4}{9}$

Lesson 7.1 Multiplying Fractions

$\frac{3}{4} \times \frac{1}{6} = \frac{3 \times 1}{4 \times 6}$ ← ---- Multiply the numerators. ----→ $\frac{2}{7} \times \frac{7}{10} = \frac{2 \times 7}{7 \times 10}$

$= \frac{3}{24}$ ← ---- Multiply the denominator. $= \frac{14}{70}$

$= \frac{1}{8}$ ← ---- Reduce to simplest form. ----→ $= \frac{1}{5}$

Multiply. Write answers in simplest form.

	a	b	c
1.	$\frac{1}{3} \times \frac{2}{9} =$ ___	$\frac{1}{8} \times \frac{2}{5} =$ ___	$\frac{3}{7} \times \frac{3}{4} =$ ___
2.	$\frac{5}{6} \times \frac{3}{8} =$ ___	$\frac{5}{9} \times \frac{3}{7} =$ ___	$\frac{6}{11} \times \frac{1}{6} =$ ___
3.	$\frac{3}{5} \times \frac{2}{3} =$ ___	$\frac{3}{7} \times \frac{1}{3} =$ ___	$\frac{1}{6} \times \frac{8}{9} =$ ___
4.	$\frac{7}{10} \times \frac{4}{5} =$ ___	$\frac{7}{8} \times \frac{2}{7} =$ ___	$\frac{1}{2} \times \frac{5}{11} =$ ___
5.	$\frac{5}{7} \times \frac{7}{9} =$ ___	$\frac{3}{4} \times \frac{9}{10} =$ ___	$\frac{7}{12} \times \frac{7}{11} =$ ___

Lesson 7.2 Multiplying Fractions and Whole Numbers

$\frac{2}{3} \times 6 = \frac{2}{3} \times \frac{6}{1}$ Rewrite the whole number as a fraction. $7 \times \frac{1}{2} = \frac{7}{1} \times \frac{1}{2}$

$= \frac{2 \times 6}{3 \times 1}$ Multiply the numerators.
Multiply the denominators. $= \frac{7 \times 1}{1 \times 2}$

$= \frac{12}{3}$ $= \frac{7}{2}$

$= 4$ Reduce to simplest form. $= 3\frac{1}{2}$

Multiply. Write answers in simplest form.

	a	b	c	d
1.	$3 \times \frac{1}{8} =$ ___	$5 \times \frac{2}{3} =$ ___	$\frac{2}{9} \times 8 =$ ___	$\frac{4}{7} \times 2 =$ ___
2.	$6 \times \frac{3}{5} =$ ___	$2 \times \frac{5}{9} =$ ___	$\frac{2}{7} \times 3 =$ ___	$7 \times \frac{3}{4} =$ ___
3.	$\frac{8}{9} \times 4 =$ ___	$\frac{1}{2} \times 8 =$ ___	$\frac{4}{5} \times 6 =$ ___	$9 \times \frac{1}{3} =$ ___
4.	$5 \times \frac{3}{10} =$ ___	$\frac{2}{3} \times 3 =$ ___	$9 \times \frac{7}{8} =$ ___	$\frac{6}{11} \times 7 =$ ___
5.	$\frac{4}{9} \times 7 =$ ___	$9 \times \frac{3}{10} =$ ___	$2 \times \frac{7}{12} =$ ___	$\frac{5}{7} \times 8 =$ ___

Lesson 7.3 Multiplying Mixed Numerals and Whole Numbers

$3 \times 2\frac{5}{6} = \frac{3}{1} \times \frac{17}{6}$ Write the whole number as a fraction.

     Write the mixed numeral as an

$= \frac{3 \times 17}{1 \times 6}$ improper fraction.

$= \frac{51}{6}$ Multiply fractions.

$= 8\frac{3}{6} = 8\frac{1}{2}$ Reduce to simplest form.

$4\frac{1}{3} \times 2 = \frac{13}{3} \times \frac{2}{1}$

$= \frac{13 \times 2}{3 \times 1}$

$= \frac{26}{3}$

$= 8\frac{2}{3}$

Multiply. Write answers in simplest form.

	a	b	c	d
1.	$1\frac{1}{5} \times 4 =$ ___	$5 \times 3\frac{2}{3} =$ ___	$4\frac{2}{7} \times 6 =$ ___	$3 \times 2\frac{2}{5} =$ ___
2.	$5\frac{1}{6} \times 7 =$ ___	$3 \times 2\frac{5}{6} =$ ___	$2 \times 9\frac{2}{3} =$ ___	$8 \times 4\frac{1}{7} =$ ___
3.	$2 \times 2\frac{3}{5} =$ ___	$1\frac{7}{12} \times 9 =$ ___	$5 \times 3\frac{1}{8} =$ ___	$7\frac{1}{4} \times 2 =$ ___
4.	$3\frac{3}{10} \times 8 =$ ___	$4 \times 2\frac{1}{2} =$ ___	$3 \times 1\frac{5}{9} =$ ___	$2\frac{7}{8} \times 2 =$ ___
5.	$6 \times 3\frac{2}{5} =$ ___	$9\frac{2}{7} \times 4 =$ ___	$7 \times 8\frac{5}{9} =$ ___	$3\frac{5}{7} \times 2 =$ ___

Lesson 7.4 Multiplying Mixed Numerals

$2\frac{1}{5} \times 1\frac{1}{4} = \frac{11}{5} \times \frac{5}{4}$ Write the mixed numerals as improper fractions.

Multiply fractions.

$= \frac{55}{20}$

$= 2\frac{15}{20} = 2\frac{3}{4}$ Write the answer in simplest form.

Multiply. Write answers in simplest form.

	a	b	c	d
1.	$2\frac{1}{4} \times 3\frac{1}{3} =$ ___	$5\frac{1}{2} \times 1\frac{1}{6} =$ ___	$3\frac{1}{4} \times 4\frac{2}{3} =$ ___	$1\frac{6}{7} \times 2\frac{2}{3} =$ ___
2.	$1\frac{7}{10} \times 4\frac{3}{4} =$ ___	$3\frac{3}{5} \times 4\frac{1}{7} =$ ___	$1\frac{5}{9} \times 3\frac{1}{2} =$ ___	$6\frac{2}{3} \times 2\frac{1}{9} =$ ___
3.	$5\frac{3}{5} \times 2\frac{1}{4} =$ ___	$6\frac{1}{3} \times 1\frac{2}{5} =$ ___	$9\frac{1}{2} \times 2\frac{2}{7} =$ ___	$2\frac{6}{7} \times 5\frac{1}{7} =$ ___
4.	$8\frac{1}{6} \times 2\frac{1}{2} =$ ___	$3\frac{1}{8} \times 1\frac{5}{8} =$ ___	$7\frac{1}{2} \times 1\frac{1}{5} =$ ___	$3\frac{5}{6} \times 3\frac{1}{5} =$ ___
5.	$1\frac{7}{12} \times 2\frac{5}{6} =$ ___	$2\frac{1}{6} \times 7\frac{1}{2} =$ ___	$2\frac{1}{8} \times 3\frac{1}{4} =$ ___	$8\frac{2}{3} \times 4\frac{1}{2} =$ ___

NAME _____

Lesson 7.5 Multiplication Practice

Multiply. Write answers in simplest form.

	a	b	c	d

1. $\dfrac{3}{5} \times \dfrac{1}{2} =$ ___ $\dfrac{4}{7} \times \dfrac{2}{3} =$ ___ $\dfrac{4}{5} \times \dfrac{5}{6} =$ ___ $\dfrac{1}{6} \times \dfrac{3}{4} =$ ___

2. $\dfrac{2}{3} \times \dfrac{1}{3} =$ ___ $4 \times \dfrac{2}{7} =$ ___ $8 \times \dfrac{1}{3} =$ ___ $2 \times \dfrac{3}{10} =$ ___

3. $\dfrac{8}{9} \times 3 =$ ___ $\dfrac{2}{5} \times 5 =$ ___ $4 \times \dfrac{3}{8} =$ ___ $3 \times 1\dfrac{2}{3} =$ ___

4. $7 \times 2\dfrac{3}{4} =$ ___ $6 \times \dfrac{1}{8} =$ ___ $1\dfrac{6}{7} \times 2\dfrac{1}{2} =$ ___ $5\dfrac{1}{4} \times 2\dfrac{1}{3} =$ ___

5. $4\dfrac{7}{9} \times 3\dfrac{1}{2} =$ ___ $2 \times 8\dfrac{3}{5} =$ ___ $9 \times 1\dfrac{1}{6} =$ ___ $6 \times 2\dfrac{7}{12} =$ ___

6. $2\dfrac{1}{8} \times 3\dfrac{1}{2} =$ ___ $4\dfrac{2}{3} \times 3\dfrac{1}{7} =$ ___ $3\dfrac{3}{5} \times 1\dfrac{5}{6} =$ ___ $3\dfrac{2}{7} \times 3\dfrac{1}{3} =$ ___

Lesson 7.6 Problem Solving

SHOW YOUR WORK

Solve each problem. Write answers in simplest form.

1. Simon bought $\frac{2}{3}$ pound of cookies. He ate $\frac{4}{5}$ of the cookies he bought. What was the weight of the cookies that Simon ate?

   Simon ate ___$\frac{8}{15}$___ pound of cookies.

2. Students must take their tests home to be signed. Two-thirds of the class took home their tests. Only $\frac{1}{8}$ of the students who took their tests home got them signed. What fraction of the entire class got their tests signed?

   ___$\frac{1}{12}$___ of the class got their tests signed.

3. One serving of pancakes calls for $\frac{1}{3}$ cup of milk. How many cups of milk are needed for 4 servings of pancakes?

   ___$1\frac{1}{3}$___ cups of milk are needed for four servings of pancakes.

4. If Carlos works $\frac{5}{12}$ of a day every day, how much will Carlos have worked after 5 days?

   After five days, Carlos will have worked ___$2\frac{1}{12}$___ days.

5. Tony had $1\frac{1}{2}$ gallons of orange juice. He drank $\frac{2}{7}$ of the orange juice he had. How much orange juice did Tony drink?

   Tony drank ___$\frac{3}{7}$___ gallon of orange juice.

6. Miranda has 3 kites. Each kite needs $4\frac{2}{3}$ yards of string. How much string does Miranda need for all 3 kites?

   Miranda needs ___14___ yards of string.

1.	2.
$\begin{array}{r} \frac{2}{3} \\ \times \frac{4}{5} \\ \hline \frac{8}{15} \end{array}$	$\begin{array}{r} \frac{2}{3} \\ \times \frac{1}{8} \\ \hline \frac{1}{12} \end{array}$
3.	4.
$\begin{array}{r} 4 \\ \times \frac{1}{3} \\ \hline 1\frac{1}{3} \end{array}$	$\begin{array}{r} 5 \\ \times \frac{5}{12} \\ \hline 2\frac{1}{12} \end{array}$
5.	6.
$\begin{array}{r} 1\frac{1}{2} \\ \times \frac{2}{7} \\ \hline \frac{3}{7} \end{array}$	$\begin{array}{r} 4\frac{2}{3} \\ \times 3 \\ \hline 14 \end{array}$

Check What You Learned

Multiplying Fractions

Multiply. Write answers in simplest form.

	a	b	c
1.	$\dfrac{1}{4} \times \dfrac{8}{9} =$ ____	$\dfrac{3}{5} \times \dfrac{5}{6} =$ ____	$\dfrac{5}{7} \times \dfrac{1}{2} =$ ____
2.	$\dfrac{11}{12} \times \dfrac{2}{3} =$ ____	$\dfrac{3}{7} \times \dfrac{4}{5} =$ ____	$\dfrac{3}{4} \times \dfrac{3}{8} =$ ____
3.	$3 \times \dfrac{5}{8} =$ ____	$4 \times \dfrac{1}{6} =$ ____	$\dfrac{1}{3} \times 9 =$ ____
4.	$\dfrac{5}{9} \times 7 =$ ____	$6 \times 1\dfrac{2}{3} =$ ____	$7\dfrac{1}{2} \times 5 =$ ____
5.	$3\dfrac{7}{12} \times 2 =$ ____	$3 \times 4\dfrac{6}{7} =$ ____	$5\dfrac{1}{2} \times 1\dfrac{5}{12} =$ ____
6.	$2\dfrac{3}{4} \times 4\dfrac{1}{2} =$ ____	$6\dfrac{1}{3} \times 1\dfrac{7}{8} =$ ____	$8\dfrac{2}{7} \times 3\dfrac{1}{6} =$ ____

CHAPTER 7 POSTTEST

Check What You Learned

Multiplying Fractions

Solve each problem. Write answers in simplest form.

7. Seven-twelfths of a new dress has been sewn. Chelsea did $\frac{3}{7}$ of the sewing. How much of the dress did Chelsea sew?

   Chelsea sewed _____ $\frac{1}{4}$ _____ of the dress.

8. For each cherry pie, Mrs. Carlson adds $1\frac{5}{7}$ cups of cherries. Mrs. Carlson baked 3 cherry pies. How many cups of cherries did she add?

   She added _____ $5\frac{1}{7}$ _____ cups of cherries.

9. The truck driver drives for $2\frac{1}{5}$ days to complete one delivery. How many days will the truck driver drive to complete 6 deliveries?

   The driver will drive for _____ $13\frac{1}{5}$ _____ days.

10. Roberto studied $\frac{3}{5}$ hour every day for 7 days. How many hours did Roberto study in 7 days?

    Roberto studied _____ $4\frac{1}{5}$ _____ hours.

11. A race track was $\frac{1}{4}$ mile long. If Martha ran around the race track $5\frac{1}{9}$ times, how many miles did Martha run?

    Martha ran _____ $1\frac{5}{18}$ _____ miles.

12. Mrs. Fernandez must drive $6\frac{1}{9}$ miles to work every day. How many miles will Mrs. Fernandez have driven after 12 days of work?

    After twelve days of work, Mrs. Fernandez will have driven _____ $73\frac{1}{3}$ _____ miles.

7.	8.
$\frac{7}{12}$ $\times \frac{3}{7}$ $\frac{1}{4}$	$1\frac{5}{7}$ $\times 3$ $5\frac{1}{7}$

9.	10.
$2\frac{1}{5}$ $\times 6$ $13\frac{1}{5}$	7 $\times \frac{3}{5}$ $4\frac{1}{5}$

11.	12.
$5\frac{1}{9}$ $\times \frac{1}{4}$ $1\frac{5}{18}$	$6\frac{1}{9}$ $\times 12$ $73\frac{1}{3}$

Check What You Know

Dividing Fractions

Divide. Write answers in simplest form.

	a	b	c	d
1.	$6 \div \dfrac{9}{10} =$ ___	$\dfrac{7}{8} \div 14 =$ ___	$\dfrac{2}{9} \div 2 =$ ___	$1 \div \dfrac{3}{4} =$ ___
2.	$\dfrac{3}{5} \div 9 =$ ___	$\dfrac{3}{4} \div 6 =$ ___	$\dfrac{7}{9} \div \dfrac{5}{6} =$ ___	$\dfrac{1}{5} \div \dfrac{2}{5} =$ ___
3.	$\dfrac{7}{8} \div \dfrac{1}{4} =$ ___	$\dfrac{7}{10} \div \dfrac{5}{8} =$ ___	$\dfrac{11}{12} \div \dfrac{3}{8} =$ ___	$\dfrac{4}{9} \div 2\dfrac{1}{2} =$ ___
4.	$3\dfrac{1}{5} \div 12 =$ ___	$2 \div 5\dfrac{1}{3} =$ ___	$8 \div 2\dfrac{2}{11} =$ ___	$\dfrac{5}{7} \div 1\dfrac{1}{4} =$ ___
5.	$5\dfrac{5}{8} \div 4\dfrac{1}{2} =$ ___	$11 \div 6\dfrac{1}{9} =$ ___	$3\dfrac{9}{11} \div 8\dfrac{2}{5} =$ ___	$7\dfrac{3}{7} \div 8\dfrac{5}{12} =$ ___

Check What You Know

SHOW YOUR WORK

Dividing Fractions

Solve each problem. Write answers in simplest form.

6. Hotah and his 3 friends are each running an equal part of a $1\frac{5}{6}$ mile relay race. How far is each person running?

Each person is running _____ mile.

7. Isabel watched a play that was $2\frac{1}{4}$ hours long. She stood up every $\frac{3}{4}$ hour to stretch her legs. How many times did Isabel stand up during the play?

Isabel stood up _____ times during the play.

8. Maria brought home a sandwich that was $6\frac{1}{8}$ feet long to share with 4 members of her family. If each person, including Maria, ate the same amount of sandwich, how many feet of the sandwich did each person eat?

Each person ate _____ feet of the sandwich.

9. Ed visited Ms. Lieu 3 times last week for a total of $5\frac{1}{10}$ hours. Ed spent the same amount of time with Ms. Lieu each visit. How long was each visit?

Each visit was _____ hours long.

10. If $2\frac{1}{7}$ gallons of water fit into 1 box, how many boxes are needed to pack $8\frac{3}{4}$ gallons of water?

_____ boxes are needed.

6.	7.
8.	**9.**
10.	

Lesson 8.1　Reciprocals

The product of 2 reciprocals is always 1.

reciprocals

$$\frac{9}{10} \times \frac{10}{9} = \frac{9 \times 10}{10 \times 9}$$

$$= \frac{90}{90} = 1$$

The reciprocal of $\frac{9}{10}$ is $\frac{10}{9}$.

The reciprocal of $\frac{10}{9}$ is $\frac{9}{10}$.

$$7 = \frac{7}{1}$$

$$\frac{7}{1} \times \frac{1}{7} = \frac{7}{7} = 1$$

The reciprocal of 7 is $\frac{1}{7}$.

The reciprocal of $\frac{1}{7}$ is 7.

Write the reciprocal. Do not change improper fractions to mixed numerals.

	a	b	c	d	e	f
1.	$\frac{4}{5}$ ___	$\frac{1}{3}$ ___	$\frac{7}{8}$ ___	$\frac{9}{10}$ ___	$\frac{3}{5}$ ___	$\frac{4}{7}$ ___
2.	$\frac{3}{4}$ ___	$\frac{5}{8}$ ___	$\frac{5}{12}$ ___	$\frac{5}{3}$ ___	$\frac{1}{8}$ ___	$\frac{2}{3}$ ___
3.	9 ___	$\frac{10}{7}$ ___	$\frac{1}{5}$ ___	$\frac{9}{2}$ ___	$\frac{3}{2}$ ___	6 ___
4.	$\frac{7}{9}$ ___	$\frac{8}{1}$ ___	$\frac{12}{7}$ ___	2 ___	$\frac{1}{9}$ ___	$\frac{11}{12}$ ___
5.	$\frac{1}{11}$ ___	$\frac{9}{5}$ ___	5 ___	$\frac{8}{5}$ ___	9 ___	$\frac{5}{7}$ ___
6.	$\frac{7}{12}$ ___	$\frac{15}{1}$ ___	$\frac{5}{2}$ ___	$\frac{7}{1}$ ___	$\frac{11}{7}$ ___	$\frac{3}{17}$ ___
7.	$\frac{1}{14}$ ___	11 ___	13 ___	$\frac{15}{4}$ ___	$\frac{5}{16}$ ___	12 ___
8.	4 ___	$\frac{5}{4}$ ___	$\frac{11}{4}$ ___	$\frac{1}{12}$ ___	$\frac{7}{6}$ ___	$\frac{11}{10}$ ___
9.	$\frac{3}{1}$ ___	$\frac{4}{19}$ ___	16 ___	$\frac{8}{11}$ ___	$\frac{5}{1}$ ___	$\frac{18}{11}$ ___

Lesson 8.2 Dividing Whole Numbers and Fractions

Multiply by the reciprocal.

$$\frac{2}{3} \div 6 = \frac{2}{3} \times \frac{1}{6}$$

$$= \frac{2 \times 1}{3 \times 6}$$ Multiply the fractions.

$$= \frac{2}{18} = \frac{1}{9}$$ Write the answer in simplest form.

Multiply by the reciprocal.

$$6 \div \frac{3}{8} = \frac{6}{1} \times \frac{8}{3}$$

$$= \frac{6 \times 8}{1 \times 3}$$

$$= \frac{48}{3}$$

$$= 16$$

Divide. Write answers in simplest form.

	a	b	c	d
1.	$\frac{2}{3} \div 3 = $ ___	$4 \div \frac{3}{5} = $ ___	$\frac{4}{5} \div 8 = $ ___	$\frac{5}{6} \div 5 = $ ___
2.	$\frac{5}{8} \div 3 = $ ___	$5 \div \frac{1}{3} = $ ___	$4 \div \frac{2}{5} = $ ___	$\frac{2}{3} \div 12 = $ ___
3.	$10 \div \frac{10}{11} = $ ___	$\frac{4}{7} \div 2 = $ ___	$4 \div \frac{7}{12} = $ ___	$\frac{5}{9} \div 10 = $ ___
4.	$6 \div \frac{2}{9} = $ ___	$\frac{5}{6} \div 9 = $ ___	$3 \div \frac{3}{7} = $ ___	$\frac{3}{4} \div 12 = $ ___

Lesson 8.3 Dividing Fractions by Fractions

reciprocals

$$\frac{1}{6} \div \frac{4}{9} = \frac{1}{6} \times \frac{9}{4} \qquad \frac{9}{4} \text{ is the reciprocal of } \frac{4}{9}.$$

$$= \frac{1 \times 9}{6 \times 4} \qquad \text{Multiply by the reciprocal.}$$

$$= \frac{9}{24} = \frac{3}{8} \qquad \text{Reduce to simplest form.}$$

Divide. Write answers in simplest form.

	a	b	c	d
1.	$\frac{1}{3} \div \frac{1}{2} =$ _____	$\frac{4}{5} \div \frac{1}{10} =$ _____	$\frac{7}{12} \div \frac{7}{8} =$ _____	$\frac{3}{8} \div \frac{1}{4} =$ _____
2.	$\frac{5}{9} \div \frac{2}{3} =$ _____	$\frac{1}{6} \div \frac{1}{4} =$ _____	$\frac{2}{5} \div \frac{4}{7} =$ _____	$\frac{9}{10} \div \frac{2}{5} =$ _____
3.	$\frac{5}{7} \div \frac{1}{6} =$ _____	$\frac{2}{3} \div \frac{8}{9} =$ _____	$\frac{2}{3} \div \frac{1}{3} =$ _____	$\frac{1}{4} \div \frac{3}{8} =$ _____
4.	$\frac{4}{5} \div \frac{3}{10} =$ _____	$\frac{5}{12} \div \frac{10}{11} =$ _____	$\frac{7}{8} \div \frac{6}{7} =$ _____	$\frac{5}{8} \div \frac{7}{10} =$ _____

Lesson 8.4 Dividing Mixed Numerals

$$2\frac{5}{8} \div 3 = \frac{21}{8} \div \frac{3}{1}$$

Write mixed numerals as improper fractions.

$$= \frac{21}{8} \times \frac{1}{3}$$

Multiply by the reciprocal.

$$= \frac{21}{24}$$

$$= \frac{7}{8}$$

Reduce to simplest form.

$$4\frac{7}{8} \div 5\frac{1}{5} = \frac{39}{8} \div \frac{26}{5}$$

$$= \frac{39}{8} \times \frac{5}{26}$$

$$= \frac{195}{208}$$

$$= \frac{15}{16}$$

Divide. Write answers in simplest form.

	a	b	c	d

1. $3\frac{1}{2} \div 4 = $ _____ $2\frac{1}{3} \div 7 = $ _____ $5\frac{1}{9} \div 7\frac{2}{3} = $ _____ $1\frac{1}{2} \div 8\frac{1}{4} = $ _____

2. $2\frac{4}{5} \div 7 = $ _____ $4 \div 1\frac{1}{3} = $ _____ $8 \div 5\frac{1}{3} = $ _____ $5 \div 4\frac{1}{6} = $ _____

3. $2\frac{5}{8} \div 1\frac{1}{2} = $ _____ $2\frac{1}{7} \div 3 = $ _____ $2\frac{7}{9} \div 4\frac{2}{7} = $ _____ $3\frac{1}{7} \div 6\frac{3}{5} = $ _____

Lesson 8.5 Division Practice

Divide. Write answers in simplest form.

a b c d

1. $\dfrac{1}{2} \div 7 =$ _____ $\dfrac{1}{4} \div 9 =$ _____ $\dfrac{2}{3} \div 8 =$ _____ $5 \div \dfrac{10}{11} =$ _____

2. $3 \div \dfrac{4}{5} =$ _____ $\dfrac{3}{8} \div \dfrac{9}{10} =$ _____ $\dfrac{1}{12} \div \dfrac{6}{11} =$ _____ $\dfrac{3}{4} \div 6 =$ _____

3. $\dfrac{2}{3} \div \dfrac{4}{5} =$ _____ $\dfrac{3}{14} \div \dfrac{2}{7} =$ _____ $\dfrac{1}{6} \div \dfrac{4}{9} =$ _____ $5\dfrac{1}{3} \div 2\dfrac{2}{3} =$ _____

4. $4 \div 2\dfrac{2}{5} =$ _____ $3\dfrac{1}{8} \div 7\dfrac{1}{2} =$ _____ $5\dfrac{3}{5} \div 8\dfrac{5}{9} =$ _____ $6\dfrac{2}{7} \div 6\dfrac{2}{9} =$ _____

5. $7\dfrac{3}{9} \div \dfrac{9}{11} =$ _____ $8 \div 4\dfrac{2}{5} =$ _____ $3\dfrac{5}{9} \div 9\dfrac{3}{5} =$ _____ $2\dfrac{1}{6} \div 4\dfrac{1}{3} =$ _____

Lesson 8.6 Problem Solving

SHOW YOUR WORK

Solve each problem. Write answers in simplest form.

1. Howard read $\frac{1}{6}$ of a book each day until $\frac{7}{8}$ of the book was finished. How many days has Howard been reading?

   Howard has been reading for _____ days.

2. There are 6 class periods in one school day. Each school day is $\frac{3}{7}$ day long. If each class lasts for the same part of the day, what fraction of a day is each class period?

   Each class period is _____ of a day long.

3. Janet has 8 ounces of coffee beans. If each pot of coffee requires $\frac{5}{9}$ ounce of coffee beans, how many pots of coffee can Janet make?

   Janet can make _____ pots of coffee.

4. A recipe for four dozen cookies requires $1\frac{1}{2}$ cups of flour. How much flour is needed for one dozen cookies?

   One dozen cookies requires _____ cup of flour.

5. Keith has $7\frac{1}{8}$ yards of string. He needs $1\frac{5}{7}$ yards of string for each of his kites. How many kites can Keith make with his string? Write the remainder as a fraction.

   Keith can make _____ kites.

6. Mr. Garcia worked $7\frac{1}{5}$ hours on Wednesday. He took a break every $3\frac{3}{5}$ hours. How many breaks did Mr. Garcia take?

   Mr. Garcia took _____ breaks on Wednesday.

1.	2.
3.	4.
5.	6.

Check What You Learned

Dividing Fractions

Divide. Write answers in simplest form.

	a	b	c	d

1. $6 \div \dfrac{1}{8} =$ _____ $2 \div \dfrac{3}{10} =$ _____ $\dfrac{8}{9} \div 4 =$ _____ $\dfrac{2}{3} \div 10 =$ _____

2. $\dfrac{3}{7} \div \dfrac{9}{14} =$ _____ $\dfrac{2}{5} \div 4 =$ _____ $\dfrac{12}{14} \div \dfrac{6}{7} =$ _____ $\dfrac{5}{6} \div \dfrac{9}{10} =$ _____

3. $\dfrac{9}{11} \div \dfrac{3}{11} =$ _____ $\dfrac{1}{6} \div \dfrac{2}{9} =$ _____ $2\dfrac{1}{3} \div \dfrac{7}{8} =$ _____ $1\dfrac{4}{5} \div 6 =$ _____

4. $\dfrac{5}{8} \div 3\dfrac{1}{8} =$ _____ $1\dfrac{2}{7} \div 12 =$ _____ $5 \div 3\dfrac{1}{3} =$ _____ $2\dfrac{5}{8} \div 8\dfrac{2}{5} =$ _____

5. $7 \div 4\dfrac{3}{4} =$ _____ $5\dfrac{1}{9} \div 8\dfrac{7}{9} =$ _____ $6\dfrac{2}{3} \div 8\dfrac{4}{7} =$ _____ $1\dfrac{5}{9} \div 9\dfrac{1}{2} =$ _____

Solve each problem. Write answers in simplest form.

6. Three friends ate $\frac{3}{4}$ of a pizza. The 3 friends ate equal amounts. How much of the pizza did each friend eat?

   Each friend ate _____ of the pizza.

7. Andrew must cut a rope $9\frac{1}{7}$ yards long into 8 equal pieces. How long will each piece of rope be?

   Each piece of rope will be _____ yards long.

8. Emily received 19 stickers for all the homework assignments she completed. Emily completed $6\frac{1}{3}$ assignments. She received the same number of stickers for each homework assignment. How many stickers did Emily receive for each assignment?

   Emily received _____ stickers for each assignment.

9. Choir practice lasts $2\frac{1}{3}$ hours each week. How many weeks will the choir have practiced after $9\frac{4}{5}$ hours?

   The choir will have practiced for _____ weeks.

10. Keisha's guitar lessons are $1\frac{2}{9}$ hours long. After $12\frac{5}{6}$ hours, how many guitar lessons has Keisha had?

    Keisha has had _____ guitar lessons.

11. Ms. Perez bought $4\frac{9}{10}$ ounces of seed for 14 gardens. If each garden gets an equal amount of seed, how many ounces of seed will be in each garden?

    Each garden will have _____ ounce of seed.

6.	7.
8.	**9.**
10.	**11.**

Check What You Know

Customary Measurement

Complete the following.

	a	b

1. 6 ft. = _____ yd.   3 mi. = _____ ft.

2. 84 in. = _____ ft.   4 yd. = _____ in.

3. 8 ft. 9 in. = _____ in.   2 mi. 3,400 ft. = _____ ft.

4. 4 qt. = _____ pt.   13 pt. = _____ c.

5. 5 gal. = _____ qt.   3 qt. = _____ c.

6. 3 gal. 3 qt. = _____ qt.   6 qt. 1 pt. = _____ pt.

7. 3 lb. = _____ oz.   144 oz. = _____ lb.

8. 16,000 lb. = _____ T.   2 T. 1,550 lb. = _____ lb.

9. 8 lb. 5 oz. = _____ oz.   12 lb. 2 oz. = _____ oz.

Find the perimeter of each figure.

10.

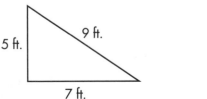

_____ feet

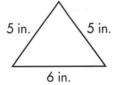

_____ inches

11.

_____ feet

_____ yards

NAME **Victoria Kwei**

Check What You Know

Customary Measurement

Find the area of each rectangle.

	a		b

12.

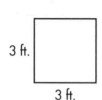

3 ft.

3 ft.

_____9_____ square feet

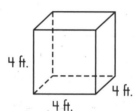

2 yd.

8 yd.

_____16_____ square yards

Fine the volume of each rectangular solid.

13.

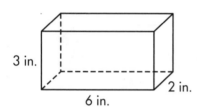

3 in.

6 in.   2 in.

_____36_____ cubic inches

4 ft.

4 ft.   4 ft.

_____64_____ cubic feet

SHOW YOUR WORK

Answer the following questions.

14. Mr. Woodson built a rectangular fence around his yard. The fence is 60 feet long and 35 feet wide. What is the area of the yard?

The area of the yard is _____2,100_____ square feet.

14.
```
   60
 × 35
 ────
 2,100
```

15. Angelica is wrapping a present in a rectangular box. The box is 6 inches in height, 20 inches in length, and 10 inches in width. What is the volume of the box?

The volume of the box is _____1,200_____ cubic inches.

15.
```
   20
   10
  × 6
 ────
 1,200
```

Lesson 9.1   Units of Length (inches, feet, yards, and miles)

| 1 foot (ft.) = 12 inches (in.)   1 yard (yd.) = 3 feet (ft.) = 36 inches (in.) |
| 1 mile (mi.) = 5,280 feet (ft.) = 1,760 yards (yd.) |

48 in. = ___ ft.   2 yd. 2 ft. = ___ ft.

12 in. = 1 ft.   1 yd. = 3 ft.
                                    2 yd. = 2 × 3 ft. = 6 ft.

12 in. × 4 = 48 in.   2 yd. 2 ft. = 6 ft. + 2 ft.

48 in. = __4__ ft.   2 yd. 2 ft. = __8__ ft.

Complete the following.

	a	b	c
1.	12 ft. = ____ yd.	120 in. = ____ ft.	3 yd. = ____ ft.
2.	6 yd. = ____ ft.	2 mi. = ____ ft.	27 ft. = ____ yd.
3.	36 in. = ____ yd.	10 ft. = ____ in.	1 mi. = ____ yd.
4.	4 ft. 9 in. = ____ in.	9 yd. = ____ ft.	2 mi. 722 ft. = ____ ft.
5.	1 yd. = ____ in.	4 yd. 2 ft. = ____ ft.	324 in. = ____ yd.
6.	8 ft. 2 in. = ____ in.	18 ft. = ____ yd.	2 yd. = ____ in.
7.	4 yd. = ____ in.	5 ft. = ____ in.	96 in. = ____ ft.
8.	1 mi. 347 ft. = ____ ft.	4 mi. = ____ yd.	1 yd. 2 ft. = ____ ft.
9.	7 yd. = ____ in.	1 yd. 72 in. = ____ yd.	11 ft. 2 in. = ____ in.
10.	3 yd. 8 in. = ____ in.	1 mi. 2 yd. = ____ ft.	72 in. = ____ yd.
11.	2 mi. 3,241 ft. = ____ ft.	3 yd. 1 ft. = ____ ft.	1 mi. 4 yd. = ____ yd.
12.	3 yd. 12 ft. = ____ yd.	3 yd. 7 ft. = ____ ft.	5 yd. 2 in. = ____ in.

Lesson 9.2   Liquid Volume (cups, pints, quarts, and gallons)

| 1 pint (pt.) = 2 cups (c.)   1 quart (qt.) = 2 pt. |
| 1 gallon (gal.) = 4 quarts (qt.) |

8 pt. = ___ c.   8 pt. = ___ qt.   3 gal. = ___ qt.

1 pt. = 2 c.   2 pt. = 1 qt.   1 gal. = 4 qt.
8 pt. = (8 × 2) c.   8 pt. = (8 ÷ 2) qt.   3 gal. = (3 × 4) qt.

8 pt. = _16_ c.   8 pt. = _4_ qt.   3 gal. = _12_ qt.

Complete the following.

	a	b	c
1.	6 c. = ___ pt.	8 c. = ___ qt.	4 pt. = ___ c.
2.	10 pt. = ___ qt.	9 pt. = ___ c.	3 qt. = ___ pt.
3.	2 gal. = ___ qt.	3 qt. = ___ c.	3 pt. = ___ c.
4.	7 qt. = ___ c.	2 gal. = ___ pt.	1 gal. = ___ c.
5.	3 qt. 1 pt. = ___ pt.	4 gal. = ___ qt.	2 gal. 1 qt. = ___ qt.
6.	4 qt. = ___ c.	1 qt. 1 c. = ___ c.	3 gal. = ___ c.
7.	21 pt. 1 c. = ___ c.	1 gal. 7 c. = ___ c.	6 qt. 3 c. = ___ c.
8.	8 gal. = ___ pt.	2 gal. 8 pt. = ___ gal.	3 pt. 6 c. = ___ pt.
9.	4 gal. 3 qt. = ___ qt.	3 qt. 2 c. = ___ c.	8 qt. 1 pt. = ___ pt.
10.	5 qt. = ___ c.	2 qt. 3 c. = ___ c.	9 qt. 4 pt. = ___ qt.
11.	7 qt. 2 c. = ___ c.	1 gal. 4 pt. = ___ pt.	1 gal. 7 pt. = ___ c.
12.	3 gal. 3 pt. = ___ pt.	5 qt. 2 c. = ___ c.	2 gal. 4 c. = ___ c.

Lesson 9.3 Weight (ounces, pounds, and tons)

1 pound (lb.) = 16 ounces (oz.)	2,000 pounds (lb.) = 1 ton (T.)

112 oz. = ____ lb.

16 oz. = 1 lb.
112 oz. = (112 ÷ 16) lb.

112 oz. = __7__ lb.

2 lb. 12 oz. = ____ oz.

1 lb. = 16 oz.
2 lb. = (2 × 16) oz. = 32 oz.
2 lb. 12 oz. = 32 oz. + 12 oz.

2 lb. 12 oz. = __44__ oz.

16,000 lb. = ____ T.

16,000 lb. = (16,000 ÷ 2,000) lb.

16,000 lb. = __8__ T.

Complete the following.

	a	b	c
1.	2 lb. = ____ oz.	32 oz. = ____ lb.	4 T. = ____ lb.
2.	7 T. = ____ lb.	7 lb. = ____ oz.	48 oz. = ____ lb.
3.	80 oz. = ____ lb.	1 T. = ____ oz.	2 T. = ____ lb.
4.	5 lb. = ____ oz.	1 T. 350 lb. = ____ lb.	10 T. = ____ lb.
5.	14,000 lb. = ____ T.	8 lb. = ____ oz.	1 lb. 5 oz. = ____ oz.
6.	3 lb. 3 oz. = ____ oz.	160 oz. = ____ lb.	2 T. 792 lb. = ____ lb.
7.	1 T. 5 oz. = ____ oz.	144 oz. = ____ lb.	28,000 lb. = ____ T.
8.	128,000 oz. = ____ T.	3 lb. 7 oz. = ____ lb.	5 T. = ____ oz.
9.	2 lb. 8 oz. = ____ oz.	3 T. 1,240 lb. = ____ lb.	30,000 lb. = ____ T.
10.	12 lb. 5 oz. = ____ oz.	10 T. 1,344 lb. = ____ lb.	3 T. 822 oz. = ____ oz.

Lesson 9.4 Temperature

Temperature is measured using a thermometer.

20 degrees = 20°

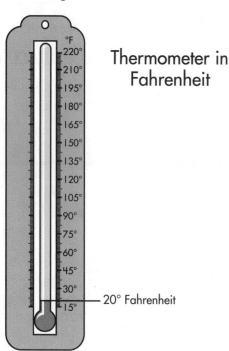

Thermometer in Fahrenheit

— 20° Fahrenheit

Fahrenheit Temperatures to remember:

32 degrees = water freezes

212 degrees = water boils

98.6 degrees = normal body temperature

Mark the following points on the blank thermometers.

1.

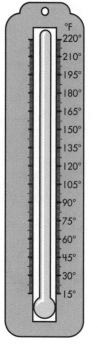

water freezes

2.

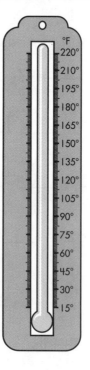

normal body temperature

3.

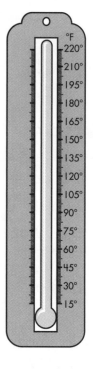

water boils

Lesson 9.5 Elapsed Time

To calculate the amount of time that has elapsed, follow these steps:
1. Count the number of whole hours between the starting time and finishing time.
2. Count the remaining minutes.
3. Add the hours and minutes.

For example: start time: 9:39 a.m.
finish time: 4:16 p.m.
From 9:39 a.m. to 3:39 p.m., count 6 hours.
From 3:39 p.m. to 4:16 p.m., count 37 minutes.
The total time elapsed is 6 hours 37 minutes.

Determine how much time has elapsed in each problem.

a   b

1.

Time elapsed: Time elapsed:

____ hours ____ minutes   ____ hours ____ minutes

2.

Arrival:	6:12 p.m.
Departure:	1:17 a.m.

Time elapsed:

____ hours ____ minutes

Departure:	2:57 p.m.
Arrival:	9:21 p.m.

Time elapsed:

____ hours ____ minutes

3.

Time start: ____ a.m.

Time finish: ____ a.m.

Time elapsed: _____

Time start: ____ p.m.

Time finish: ____ p.m.

Time elapsed: _____

Lesson 9.6   Problem Solving

Solve each problem.

1. Sonia has 1 gallon 9 cups of milk. How many cups of milk does Sonia have?

   Sonia has _____ cups of milk.

2. Each piece of candy weighs 2 ounces. Colin placed 32 pieces of candy in a bag. How much does the bag of candy weigh?

   The bag of candy weighs _____ ounces.

   The bag of candy weighs _____ pounds.

3. The fuel tank on Shannon's car holds 16 gallons of gas. There are 37 quarts of gas in the fuel tank. How many more quarts are needed to fill the fuel tank?

   The fuel tank needs _____ more quarts.

4. Rachel hiked 850 yards. Benny hiked 2,145 feet. How much farther did Rachel hike?

   Rachel hiked _____ feet. Rachel hiked _____ feet farther than Benny.

   Benny hiked _____ yards. Rachel hiked _____ yards farther than Benny.

5. An elevator can hold up to 1,800 pounds. There are 19,000 ounces on the elevator. How many more ounces can the elevator hold?

   The most weight the elevator can hold is _____ ounces.

   The elevator can hold _____ more ounces.

6. Akira began work at 8:03 a.m. He finished at 4:35 p.m. How long did Akira work?

   Akira worked for _____ hours _____ minutes.

1.	2.
3.	4.
5.	6.

Lesson 9.7   Measuring Perimeter

The **perimeter** is the sum of the sides of a figure.

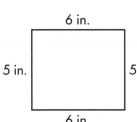

6    $6 \times 2 = 12$ To find the perimeter, add the length
5 or $5 \times 2 = 10$ of the sides.
6
+ 5
―――
2 2

1 2
+1 0
―――
2 2   The perimeter of the rectangle is __22__ in.

Find the perimeter of each figure.

        a   b   c

1.

6 in. / 4 in. / 4 in. / 6 in.   ____ in.

7 yd. / 7 yd. / 5 yd.   ____ yd.

8 ft. / 8 ft. / 2 ft. / 2 ft. / 6 ft. / 6 ft.   ____ ft.

2.

8 ft. / 9 ft. / 3 ft.   ____ ft.

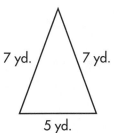

4 in. / 4 in. / 4 in. / 4 in. / 4 in. / 4 in. / 4 in. / 4 in. / 4 in. / 4 in. / 4 in. / 4 in.   ____ in.

6 in. / 6 in. / 6 in. / 6 in.   ____ in.

3.

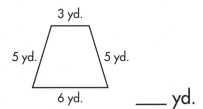

3 yd. / 5 yd. / 5 yd. / 6 yd.   ____ yd.

7 yd. / 2 yd. / 2 yd. / 7 yd.   ____ yd.

5 yd. / 3 yd. / 4 yd.   ____ yd.

4.

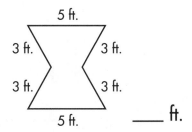

5 ft. / 3 ft. / 3 ft. / 3 ft. / 3 ft. / 5 ft.   ____ ft.

3 in. / 3 in. / 1 in. / 2 in. / 2 in. / 4 in. / 5 in. / 5 in.   ____ in.

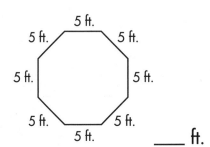

5 ft. / 5 ft. / 5 ft. / 5 ft. / 5 ft. / 5 ft. / 5 ft. / 5 ft.   ____ ft.

Lesson 9.8 Measuring Area

Area is the number of square units needed to cover a surface.

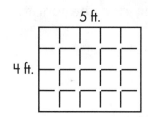

Length: 5 ft.
Width: 4 ft.

$$\begin{array}{r} 5\ \text{ft.} \\ \times\ 4\ \text{ft.} \\ \hline 2\,0\ \text{square feet} \end{array}$$

To calculate the area of a square or rectangle, multiply the measure of the length by the measure of the width.

The area of a rectangle 5 feet in length and 4 feet in width is __20 square feet__.

Find the area of each rectangle.

	a	b	c

1.

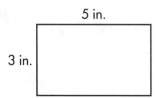
5 in.
3 in.

_____ sq. in.

4 ft.
4 ft.

_____ sq. ft.

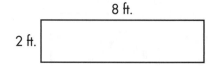
8 ft.
2 ft.

_____ sq. ft.

2.

7 yd.
2 yd.

_____ sq. yd.

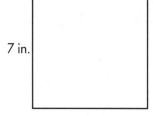
7 in.
7 in.

_____ sq. in.

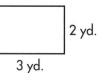
2 yd.
3 yd.

_____ sq. yd.

3.

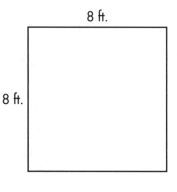
8 ft.
8 ft.

_____ sq. ft.

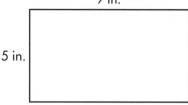
9 in.
5 in.

_____ sq. in.

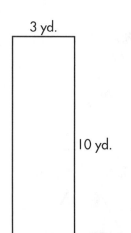
3 yd.
10 yd.

_____ sq. yd.

Lesson 9.9 Measuring Volume

Volume is the number of cubic units needed to fill a given solid.

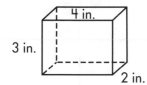

Length: 4 in.
Width: 2 in.
Height: 3 in.

Volume = length × width × height
Volume = (4 in.) × (2 in.) × (3 in.)

Volume = <u>24</u> cubic inches

Find the volume of each rectangular solid.

a	b	c

1.
 2 in. 2 in. 2 in.

_____ cu. in.

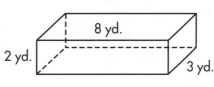 8 yd. 2 yd. 3 yd.

_____ cu. yd.

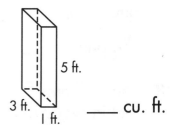 5 ft. 3 ft. 1 ft.

_____ cu. ft.

2.
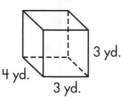 3 yd. 4 yd. 3 yd.

_____ cu. yd.

7 ft. 2 ft. 9 ft.

_____ cu. ft.

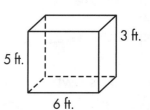 3 ft. 5 ft. 6 ft.

_____ cu. ft.

3.
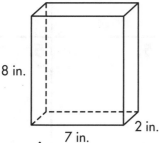 8 in. 7 in. 2 in.

_____ cu. in.

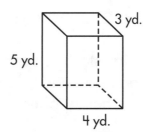 3 yd. 5 yd. 4 yd.

_____ cu. yd.

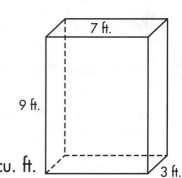 7 ft. 9 ft. 3 ft.

_____ cu. ft.

Find the volume of each rectangular solid with the given measurements.

4.

length: 7 yd.
width: 2 yd.
height: 4 yd.

_____ cu. yd.

length: 3 ft.
width: 6 ft.
height: 8 ft.

_____ cu. ft.

length: 5 in.
width: 4 in.
height: 7 in.

_____ cu. in.

Lesson 9.10 Problem Solving

Solve each problem.

1. Mr. Peate is building a rectangular fence around his house. The fence will be 32 feet long and 29 feet wide. What will be the perimeter of the fence?

   The perimeter will be _____ feet.

2. Sherman developed a photo 4 inches wide by 6 inches in length. What is the area of the photograph?

   The photo is _____ square inches.

3. The Williams family bought a house 4,560 square feet in area. The house is 60 feet long. How wide is the house?

   The house is _____ feet wide.

4. Ms. Ferris owns a barn 12 yards long, 9 yards high, and 11 yards wide. If Ms. Ferris's barn is rectangular, what is the volume of her barn?

   The volume of her barn is _____ cubic yards.

5. The storage center sells rectangular storage spaces that are each 200 cubic feet. Each space is 5 feet long and 5 feet wide. What is the height of each storage space?

   Each storage space is _____ feet high.

6. A toy doll was sent to Lucy in a box 8 inches long, 5 inches wide, and 15 inches high. What is the volume of the box?

   The volume of the box is _____ cubic inches.

1.	2.
3.	4.
5.	6.

Check What You Learned

Customary Measurement

Complete the following.

	a	b
1.	9 yd. = _____ ft.	108 in. = _____ yd.
2.	228 in. = _____ ft.	7 ft. 9 in. = _____ in.
3.	4 mi. 200 ft. = _____ ft.	2 mi. 500 yd. = _____ yd.
4.	17 pt. = _____ c.	96 c. = _____ qt.
5.	18 qt. = _____ pt.	18 qt. 1 pt. = _____ pt.
6.	8 gal. 2 qt. = _____ qt.	15 pt. 1 c. = _____ c.
7.	12 lb. = _____ oz.	112 oz. = _____ lb.
8.	14 T. = _____ lb.	4 lb. 11 oz. = _____ oz.
9.	10 lb. 10 oz. = _____ oz.	1 T. 1,856 lb. = _____ lb.

Calculate how much time has elapsed in each problem.

10.

Departure:	7:25 a.m.
Arrival:	3:42 p.m.

_____ hours _____ minutes

Departure:	6:15 p.m.
Arrival:	8:28 a.m.

_____ hours _____ minutes

Find the perimeter of each figure.

11.

6 ft.

7 ft.

_____ feet

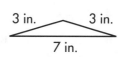

3 in.   3 in.

7 in.

_____ inches

Check What You Learned

Customary Measurement

Find the area of each rectangle.

a   b

12.

6 in.

2 in.

___12___ square inches

8 ft.

9 ft.

___72___ square feet

Find the volume of each rectangular solid.

13.

3 ft.
3 ft. 2 ft.

___18___ cubic feet

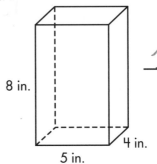

8 in.

5 in. 4 in.

___160___ cubic inches

SHOW YOUR WORK

Answer the following questions.

14. Sandra arrived at school at 7:37 a.m. She left school at 4:32 p.m. How long did Sandra stay at school?

Sandra stayed at school for ___8___ hours ___55___ minutes.

15. Charlie mowed his neighbor's lawn. The lawn is 7 yards long and 5 yards wide. How large an area did Charlie mow?

Charlie mowed ___35___ square yards.

14.

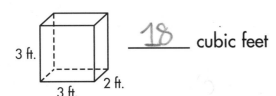

7:37 AM
(= 8 HOURS
3:37 PM
(=55 MINUTES
4:32 PM

8 H +
55 M

15.

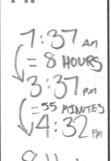

7
× 5
___
35

Check What You Know

Metric Measurement

Complete the following.

	a	b	c
1.	500 mm = _____ cm	8 km = _____ m	5,000 m = _____ mm
2.	300 cm = _____ m	300,000 cm = _____ km	3 km 200 m = _____ m
3.	6 L = _____ mL	15 kL = _____ L	4 kL = _____ mL
4.	2,000,000 mL = _____ kL	7,000 L = _____ kL	12,000 mL = _____ L
5.	8 kg = _____ g	5 g = _____ mg	7,000 mg = _____ g
6.	17,000 g = _____ kg	36,000 g = _____ kg	3 kg 500 g = _____ g

Find the perimeter of each figure.

7.

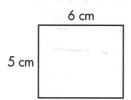

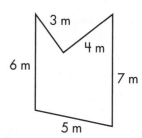

perimeter = _____ cm   perimeter = _____ km   perimeter = _____ m

NAME Victoria Kwei

Check What You Know

Metric Measurement

Find the area of each figure.

a	b	c

8.

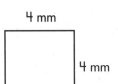
4 mm
4 mm

area = ___16___ sq. mm

1 m
1 m

area = ___1___ sq. m

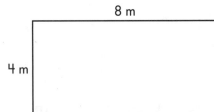
8 m
4 m

area = ___32___ sq. m

9.

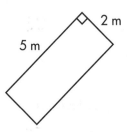
2 m
5 m

area = ___10___ sq. m

9 cm
9 cm

area = ___81___ sq. cm

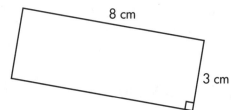
8 cm
3 cm

area = ___24___ sq. cm

Find the volume of each rectangular solid with the given measurements.

10.

length: 4 m
width: 2 m
height: 8 m

volume = _64_ cubic m

length: 7 m
width: 2 m
height: 6 m

volume = _84_ cubic m

length: 8 m
width: 8 m
height: 8 m

volume = _512_ cubic m

SHOW YOUR WORK

Answer the following question.

11. The school is standing students side-by-side to form a rectangle. If the rectangle is 20 meters long and 10 meters wide, what is its area?

The area is ___200___ square meters.

11.

```
   20
 × 10
 ─────
  200
```

Lesson 10.1 Units of Length (millimeters, centimeters, meters, and kilometers)

1 meter (m) = 100 centimeters (cm) = 1,000 millimeters (mm)
1 kilometer (km) = 1,000 m = 100,000 cm = 1,000,000 mm

3 m = ___ cm   3 m = ___ mm   4 km = ___ m
1 m = 100 cm   1 m = 1,000 mm   1 km = 1,000 m
3 m = (3 × 100) cm   3 m = (3 × 1,000) mm   4 km = (4 × 1,000) m
3 m = _300_ cm   3 m = _3,000_ mm   4 km = _4,000_ m

Complete the following.

MOCM

	a	b	c
1.	5 m = _500_ cm	20 mm = _2_ cm	2 km = _200,000_ cm
2.	7 km = _7,000_ m	3,000 m = _3_ km	200 cm = _2_ m
3.	600 mm = _60_ cm	8 m = _8,000_ mm	900 cm = _9_ m
4.	5,000 mm = _5_ m	45 cm = _450_ mm	27 m = _2,700_ cm
5.	42 m = _42,000_ mm	12 km = _12,000_ m	80 m = _80,000_ mm

Use a meterstick to measure the given objects. Round the answer to the nearest meter.

6. height of   length of a car _?_ m   height of a door _?_ m
   a classmate _?_ m

SHOW YOUR WORK

Answer each question.

7. Duane has a pencil 7 centimeters long. Fred has a pencil 64 millimeters long. Whose pencil is longer and how much longer is it?

   Duane's pencil is _6_ millimeters longer.

8. Frank bought a hose 2,800 centimeters long. How many meters long is the hose?

   The hose is _28_ meters long.

7.
70
-64
 6

8.
      28
100) 2,800

Lesson 10.2 Liquid Volume
(milliliters, liters, and kiloliters)

1 liter (L) = 1,000 milliliters (mL)   1 kiloliter (kL) = 1,000 liters (L) 1 kiloliter (kL) = 1,000,000 milliliters (mL)

3 L = ___ mL
1 L = 1,000 mL
3 L = (3 × 1,000) mL
3 L = __3,000__ mL

4 kL = ___ L
1 kL = 1,000 L
4 kL = (4 × 1,000) L
4 kL = __4,000__ L

4 kL = ___ mL
1 kL = 1,000,000 mL
4 kL = (4 × 1,000,000) mL
4 kL = __4,000,000__ mL

Complete the following.

	a	b	c
1.	3 kL = __3,000__ L	6 L = __6,000__ mL	8,000 mL = __8__ L
2.	4,000 L = __4__ kL	51,000 mL = __51__ L	5,000,000 mL = __5__ kL
3.	18 L = __18,000__ mL	2 kL = __2,000,000__ mL	22 kL = __22,000__ L
4.	4 kL = __4,000,000__ mL	46,000 L = __46__ kL	11 L = __11,000__ mL
5.	32,000 mL = __32 L__	2 L 200 mL = __2,200__ mL	12,000,000 mL = __12__ kL
6.	4 L = __4,000__ mL	3 kL 600 L = __3,600__ L	2 kL 5,000 mL = __2,005,000__ mL
7.	5 kL = __5,000__ L	16,000,000 mL = __16__ kL	8 L 772 mL = __8,772__ mL

SHOW YOUR WORK

Answer each question.

8. Nancy bought 4 liters of soda. How many milliliters of soda did Nancy buy?

Nancy bought __4,000__ milliliters of soda.

9. Jody has 7 liters of water. Marcus has 8,400 milliliters of water. How many milliliters of water does Jody have? Who has more water? How much more?

Jody has __7,000__ milliliters of water.

__Marcus__ has __1,400__ more milliliters of water.

8.
$$\begin{array}{r} 1{,}000 \\ \times \quad 4 \\ \hline 4{,}000 \end{array}$$

9.
$$\begin{array}{r} 1{,}000 \\ \times \quad 7 \\ \hline 7{,}000 \end{array}$$

$$\begin{array}{r} 8{,}400 \\ -7{,}000 \\ \hline 1{,}400 \end{array}$$

Lesson 10.3 Weight (milligrams, grams, and kilograms)

1 gram (g) = 1,000 milligrams (mg) 1 kilogram (kg) = 1,000 grams = 1,000,000 milligrams (mg)

6 g = ___ mg

1 g = 1,000 mg

6 g = (6 × 1,000) mg

6 g = __6,000__ mg

2 kg = ___ g

1 kg = 1,000 g

2 kg = (2 × 1,000) g

2 kg = __2,000__ g

Complete the following.

	a	b	c
1.	5 g = _5,000_ mg	17,000,000 mg = _17_ kg	2 kg = _200000_ mg
2.	4 kg = _4,000_ g	2,000 mg = _2_ g	8 kg 433,000 mg = _8433000_ mg
3.	7 kg = _100000_ mg	14 g = _14,000_ mg	18 kg = _18000_ g
4.	8,000 mg = _8_ g	25 kg = _15,000_ g	11,000 g = _11_ kg
5.	23 g = _13,000_ mg	19,000 g = _19_ kg	32,000 mg = _32_ g
6.	2 g 150 mg = _2,150_ mg	4 kg 200 g = _4,200_ g	5 g 273 mg = _5,273_ mg
7.	2 kg 821 g = _2,821_ g	3 kg = _3,000_ g	14 g 360 mg = _14,360_ mg
8.	256 g = _256,000_ mg	22 g 840 mg = _22,840_ mg	9 g = _9,000_ mg

SHOW YOUR WORK

Answer the following question.

9. Pedro has a stack of coins that weighs 85 grams. Conner has a stack of coins that weighs 64,300 milligrams. Whose stack of coins weighs more? How much more?

Pedro's stack of coins weighs _21,000_ milligrams more.

9. 85 g = 85,000 mg

$$\begin{array}{r} 85,000 \\ -64,000 \\ \hline 21,000 \end{array}$$

Lesson 10.4   Problem Solving

Solve each problem.

1. Ramón weighs 46 kilograms. Trent weighs 37,000 grams. Who weighs more? How much more?

    _____ weighs _____ grams more.

2. Curtis drove 82 kilometers in one hour. How many meters did he drive in an hour?

    Curtis drove _____ meters in one hour.

3. A North American earthworm can grow to 9 centimeters. How many millimeters can a North American earthworm grow to?

    A North American earthworm can grow to _____ millimeters.

4. A shark tank holds 236,000 liters of water. How many milliliters does the tank hold? How many kiloliters?

    The tank holds _____ milliliters.

    The tank holds _____ kiloliters.

5. Mrs. Rueben cooked 2,292 grams of pasta for a dinner party. How many milligrams of pasta did she cook?

    Mrs. Rueben cooked _____ milligrams of pasta.

6. Mr. Matsunaga bought 16 liters of punch for his son's birthday party. How many milliliters did he buy?

    Mr. Matsunaga bought _____ milliliters of punch.

1.	2.
3.	4.
5.	6.

Lesson 10.5 Temperature

Temperature is measured using a thermometer.
It can be measured in degrees Celsius (°C).

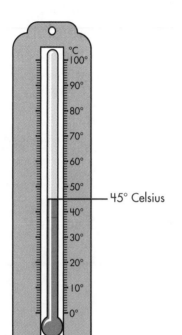

45° Celsius

Celsius Temperatures to remember:

0°C (0 degrees Celsius) = water freezes

37°C (37 degrees Celsius) = normal body temperature

100°C (100 degrees Celsius) = water boils

Mark the following points on the blank thermometers.

1.
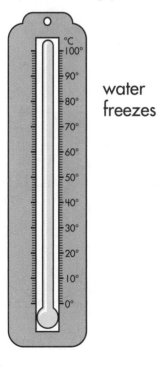
water freezes

2.
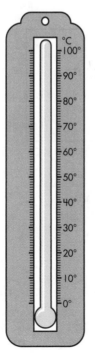
water boils

3.
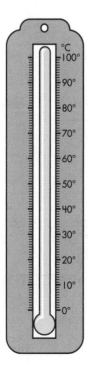
normal body temperature

Lesson 10.6 Measuring Perimeter and Area

Perimeter is the distance around an object.

To find the perimeter, add the measure of each of the sides of the triangle.

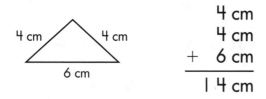

$$4 \text{ cm}$$
$$4 \text{ cm}$$
$$+ \ 6 \text{ cm}$$
$$\overline{14 \text{ cm}}$$

The perimeter of the triangle is 14 centimeters.

The **area** of an object is the number of square units needed to cover its surface.

To find the area of a rectangle, multiply the measure of its length by the measure of its width.

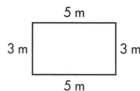

The length is 5 meters. The width is 3 meters.

Area = 5 meters × 3 meters
       = 15 square meters

The area of the rectangle is 15 square meters.

Find the perimeter of each figure.

	a	b	c

1.

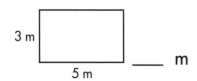 ___ m

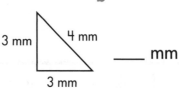 ___ mm

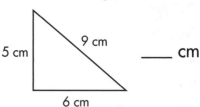 ___ cm

2.

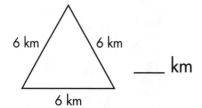 ___ km

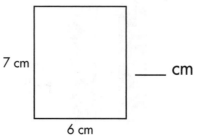 ___ cm

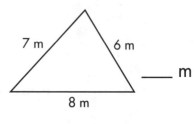 ___ m

3.

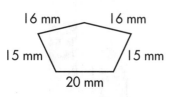 ___ mm

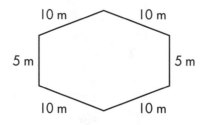 ___ m

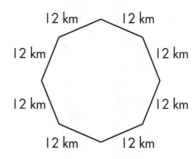 ___ km

Lesson 10.7 Measuring Volume

To find the **volume** of a rectangle, multiply the measure of its length, the measure of its width, and the measure of its height. Volume is written in cubic units.

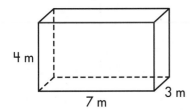

Length: 7 m
Width: 3 m
Height: 4 m

Volume = length × width × height
Volume = (7 m) × (3 m) × (4 m)

Volume = 84 cubic meters

Find the volume of each rectangular solid.

	a	b	c

1.

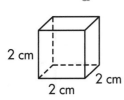

_____ cubic centimeters

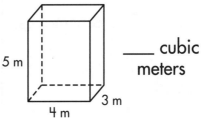

_____ cubic meters

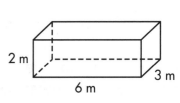

_____ cubic meters

2.

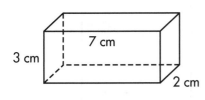

_____ cubic centimeters

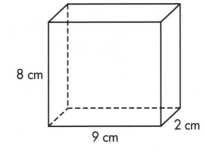

_____ cubic centimeters

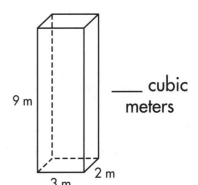

_____ cubic meters

3.

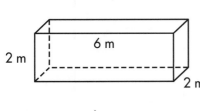

_____ cubic meters

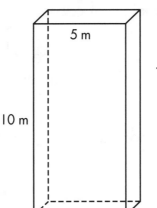

_____ cubic meters

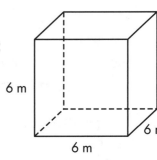

_____ cubic meters

Lesson 10.8 Problem Solving

SHOW YOUR WORK

Solve each problem.

1. A soccer field is an example of a rectangle. If a soccer field is 90 meters long and 45 meters wide, what is the perimeter of the soccer field?

   The perimeter of the field is _____ meters.

2. Julie is cutting out triangle pieces for her scrapbook. The sides of the triangle are 3 centimeters by 4 centimeters by 2 centimeters. What is the perimeter of the triangle?

   The perimeter of the triangle is _____ centimeters.

3. A town is 4 kilometers wide and 3 kilometers long. How many kilometers is it around the town?

   The perimeter is _____ kilometers.

4. Ian must mow a lawn 15 meters long and 9 meters wide. What is the area that Ian must mow?

   Ian must mow an area of _____ square meters.

5. Lea wants to put carpet on her bedroom floor. Her bedroom is 4 meters long and 6 meters wide. How much carpet does Lea need to cover the floor?

   Lea needs _____ square meters of carpet.

6. A swimming pool is 3 meters in depth, 8 meters in length, and 6 meters in width. What is the volume of the swimming pool?

   The volume of the swimming pool is _____ cubic meters.

1.	2.
3.	4.
5.	6.

NAME _____

Check What You Learned

Metric Measurement

Complete the following.

	a	b
1.	16 km = _____ m	6 m 36 cm = _____ cm
2.	8 cm 8 mm = _____ mm	4 m 850 mm = _____ mm
3.	7 kL = _____ L	10,000 mL = _____ L
4.	13 kL = _____ mL	15 L 700 mL = _____ mL
5.	22 kg = _____ g	8 g 942 mg = _____ mg

Find the perimeter of each figure.

a b

6.

perimeter = _____ mm

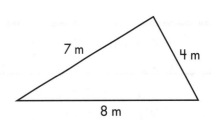

perimeter = _____ km

7.

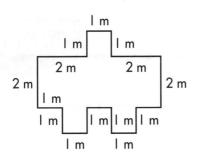

perimeter = _____ meters

perimeter = _____ meters

Check What You Learned

Metric Measurement

Complete the following.

a	b	c

8.

4 m
1 m

area =
___ square m

5 cm
3 cm

area =
___ square cm

8 cm
6 cm

area =
___ square cm

Find the volume of each rectangular solid using the given information.

9.

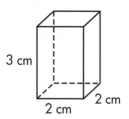

3 cm
2 cm
2 cm

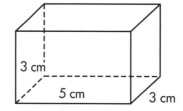

3 cm
5 cm
3 cm

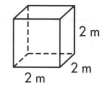

2 m
2 m
2 m

volume = ___ cubic cm   volume = ___ cubic cm   volume = ___ cubic m

10.

length: 3 mm
width: 7 mm
height: 7 mm

volume = ___ cubic mm

length: 4 m
width: 5 m
height: 5 m

volume = ___ cubic m

length: 9 cm
width: 10 cm
height: 5 cm

volume = ___ cubic cm

SHOW YOUR WORK

Answer the following question.

11. A water tank is 2 meters tall. The water tank is a rectangular solid, 5 meters long and 3 meters wide. What is its volume?

Its volume is _____ cubic meters.

11.

Check What You Know

Graphs and Probability

Answer the following questions about the bar graph.

1. How many people chose green?

_____

2. Which color was chosen by the most students? _____

3. Which color was chosen by the fewest students? _____

4. How many more students chose red than yellow? _____

5. How many people were surveyed in all? _____

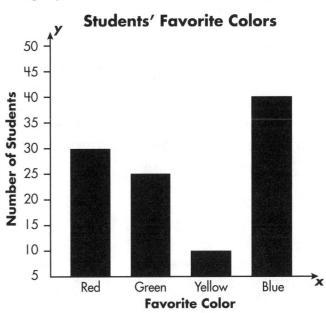

Answer the following questions about the line graph.

6. How many new garden club memberships were there in January?

_____

7. What was the total number of new memberships from October through February? _____

8. How many more new memberships were there from March through May than from October through February? _____

9. What was the total number of new memberships at the end of May?

_____

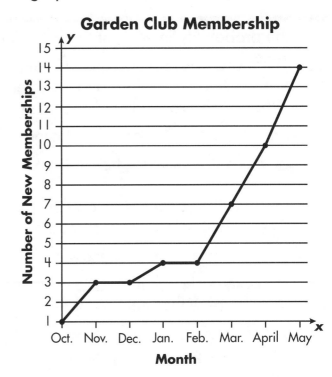

Check What You Know

Graphs and Probability

Find the mean of each set of numbers.

10. 18, 14, 23, 16, 20, 10, 18 _____

11. 280, 284, 276, 280 _____

12. 47 yd., 51 yd., 45 yd., 49 yd., 56 yd., 52 yd. _____

13. 3264, 3289, 3273, 3295, 3289 _____

Find the median, mode, and range of each set of numbers.

14. 15, 20, 10, 15, 20, 25, 20

median _____   mode _____   range _____

15. 94, 91, 98, 89, 91, 104, 91, 98, 94

median _____   mode _____   range _____

16. 821, 815, 828, 818, 815, 833, 825

median _____   mode _____   range _____

SHOW YOUR WORK

Find the probability in each of the following questions.

17. There are 36 books on a bookcase. There are 9 nonfiction, 12 fiction, and 15 science fiction. What is the probability of choosing a nonfiction book? _____ of choosing a fiction book? _____ of choosing a science fiction book? _____

18. Mrs. Watson baked an eight-layer cake, 2 layers were vanilla. What fraction of the cake is vanilla? _____ 3 layers were chocolate. What fraction of the cake is chocolate? _____ 2 layers were strawberry. What fraction of the cake is strawberry? _____ 1 layer was yellow. What fraction of the cake is yellow? _____

17.

18.

Lesson 11.1   Reading Bar Graphs

Bar graphs are used to compare different categories of information.

The bar graph here represents an elementary school's survey of the type of snack foods students prefer. The *x* axis represents the type of food. The *y* axis represents the number of students who prefer that snack food.

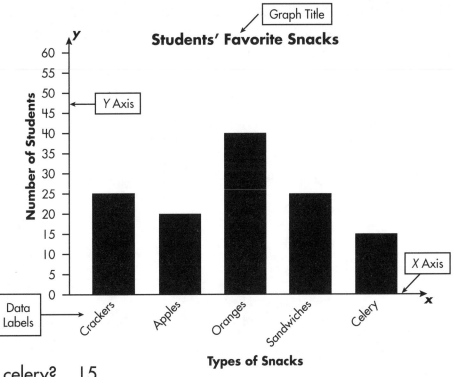

How many students chose celery? __15__

Answer the following questions about the bar graph above.

1. What are the different types of snack foods in the bar graph?

   _____

2. How many students preferred sandwiches? _____

3. How many students chose apples? _____

4. How many total students chose apples and oranges? _____

5. How many more students chose oranges than celery? _____

6. Which two snacks did the same number of students prefer? _____

7. How many total students were surveyed? _____

Lesson 11.1 Drawing a Bar Graph

Use the information in the table to draw a bar graph. Include data labels, bars, and a graph title. (Refer to page 127 for an example.) After you create the bar graph, answer the questions below.

Favorite Musical Instruments	
Instrument	Number of Students
Violin	9
Clarinet	10
Tuba	2
Viola	2
Oboe	4
Cello	7

1. What does the x axis represent? _____

2. What does the y axis represent? _____

3. Which musical instrument is preferred by the most students? _____

4. Which instruments were preferred by the same number of students?

   _____

5. How many more students prefer the violin and clarinet than the oboe and cello?

   _____

6. How many students are included in the graph data? _____

Lesson 11.2 Reading Line Graphs

Line graphs are used to show changes of quantities over time.

The horizontal axis (*x* axis) represents continuous data, usually time, and the vertical axis (*y* axis) shows the changes in quantity.

In this line graph, the *x* axis shows the months from May through October. The *y* axis shows the number of stamps collected by Shannon.

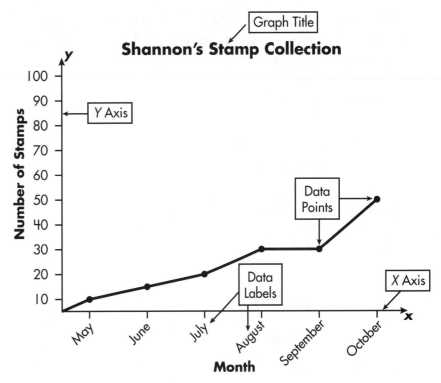

How many stamps did Shannon collect in July? __20__

How many stamps did Shannon collect during August? __30__

Refer to the line graph above and answer the following questions.

1. How many stamps had Shannon collected by the end of October? _____

2. How many stamps did Shannon collect during September? _____

3. Which months did Shannon collect the same number of stamps? _____

4. In which month did Shannon collect 10 stamps? _____

5. In which month did Shannon collect the most stamps? _____

6. How many more stamps did Shannon collect from August through October than

   from May through July? _____

Lesson 11.2 Drawing a Line Graph

Use the information in the table to draw a line graph. Include a title, data labels, lines, and data points. (See page 129 for an example.) After you create the graph, answer the questions below.

Marlon's Train Trip	
Hours of Travel	Distance Traveled Each Hour
1	32 mi.
2	50 mi.
3	85 mi.
4	85 mi.
5	105 mi.
6	130 mi.
7	110 mi.
8	85 mi.

1. What does the x axis represent? _____

2. What does the y axis represent? _____

3. In which hour did Marlon travel the greatest number of miles? _____

4. During which hour did Marlon travel the fewest miles? _____

5. Did Marlon travel a greater distance during hour 6 or hour 8? _____

6. How far did the train travel during 8 hours? _____

Lesson 11.3 Calculating the Mean

The **mean** is the average of a set of numbers. This set of numbers can be referred to as a *data set*.

Find the mean of 2, 4, 7, 8, 11, 16.

```
  1 6
  1 1                    8
    8          6) 4 8
    7          − 4 8
    4          ———
+   2              0
———
  4 8
```

To find the mean, add all of the values in the data set. Then, divide the sum by the number of values in the set.

The sum of all the numbers is 48.

There are 6 values in the set.

The mean of 2, 4, 7, 8, 11, 16 is ___8___.

Find the mean of each set of numbers.

1. 1, 3, 7, 9 _____

2. 20, 25, 29, 34 _____

3. 8, 11, 12, 17, 22 _____

4. 20, 8, 12, 15, 16, 25 _____

5. 41, 35, 32, 40 _____

6. 2 yd., 5 yd., 12 yd., 18 yd., 8 yd., 19 yd., 13 yd. _____

7. 23 in., 28 in., 36 in. _____

8. 52 m, 49 m, 58 m, 61 m _____

9. 42, 45, 32, 39, 35, 47 _____

10. 77, 82, 91, 86, 94 _____

Lesson 11.3   Problem Solving

Solve each problem.

1. The Jackson family spent $198 last week. There are three people in the family. What was the average number of dollars spent by each family member?

   Each family member spent an average of _____.

2. At a recent basketball game, the 5 starting players scored the following number of points:

   Billy: 17 points
   Vince: 24 points
   Cedric: 27 points
   Jason: 20 points
   Dijon: 12 points

   What is the mean of all the points scored?

   The mean of all points scored is _____.

3. Carson worked 5 days last week. He worked 8 hours on Monday, 12 hours on Tuesday, 8 hours on Wednesday, 7 hours on Thursday, and 10 hours on Friday. What was the average number of hours Carson worked each day last week?

   Carson worked an average of _____ each day.

4. Ezra watched 9 hours of television last week. Daniel watched 14 hours and Dixin watched 4 hours of television. What was the mean?

   They watched a mean of _____ of television.

5. Linda wrote down how many hours of sleep she got each night for seven days. She slept 4 hours on Sunday, 6 hours on Monday, 7 hours on Tuesday, 6 hours on Wednesday, 9 hours on Thursday, 5 hours on Friday, and 5 hours on Saturday. What is the mean of hours she slept each night?

   Linda slept an average of _____ each night.

1.	2.
3.	4.
5.	

Lesson 11.4 Calculating the Median, Mode, and Range

Find the median, mode, and range of 7, 6, 8, 6, 2, 5, 10.

The **median** is the value in the data set that lies in the middle of the set of data arranged in order.

> Example: Rewrite 7, 6, 8, 6, 2, 5, 10 in numerical order as
> 2, 5, 6, ⑥, 7, 8, 10. There are 7 values in the data set.
> The median is 6.

The **mode** is the value in the data set that occurs most often.

> Example: In the data set 2, 5, ⑥,⑥, 7, 8, 10, six occurs two times and the
> other values occur only once. The mode is 6.

The **range** is the difference between the largest number in the data set and the smallest number in the data set.

> Example: In the data set 2, 5, 6, 6, 7, 8, 10, the smallest number is 2 and
> the largest number is 10. The range is 8.   (10 − 2 = 8)

Find the median, mode, and range of each data set.

1. 4, 2, 9, 7, 9

median _____   mode _____   range _____

2. 7, 6, 9, 4, 4, 5, 8, 4, 7

median _____   mode _____   range _____

3. 17, 11, 8, 22, 19, 11, 10

median _____   mode _____   range _____

4. 32, 15, 24, 28, 24, 17, 24

median _____   mode _____   range _____

5. $27, $38, $21, $25, $38

median _____   mode _____   range _____

6. 2 mi., 8 mi., 9 mi., 2 mi., 2 mi., 5 mi., 5 mi.

median _____   mode _____   range _____

7. 175, 163, 157, 163, 168

median _____   mode _____   range _____

8. $74, $64, $69, $77, $71, $64, $71, $71, $75, $74, $79

median _____   mode _____   range _____

Lesson 11.4 Problem Solving

Solve each problem.

1. The heights of 5 classmates are 52 inches, 54 inches, 62 inches, 58 inches, and 58 inches. What are the median, mode, and range of the 5 heights?

   The median is _____.

   The mode is _____.

   The range is _____.

1.

2. In his last 9 basketball games, Horace scored the following number of points: 11, 16, 24, 22, 18, 22, 11, 22, and 16. What are the median, mode, and range of Horace's scores?

   The median is _____.

   The mode is _____.

   The range is _____.

2.

3. There are 5 hair salons in the town of Deerfield. The price of a basic haircut at the five salons is $12, $16, $18, $12, and $22. What are the median, mode, and range of the prices for the five salons?

   The median is _____.

   The mode is _____.

   The range is _____.

3.

4. Chan is looking for a graphing calculator at 5 different stores. The prices at the 5 stores are $108, $98, $108, $105, and $96. What are the median, mode, and range of the prices?

   The median is _____.

   The mode is _____.

   The range is _____.

4.

Lesson 11.5 Calculating Probability

Probability is the chance of an event occurring. The outcome is whether the event occurred or not.

To calculate the probability, divide the number of desired outcomes by the number of possible outcomes.

There are 6 possible outcomes of spinning the wheel.

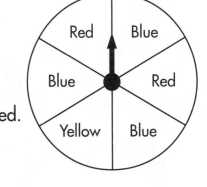

$$\text{The probability of the arrow pointing toward red} = \frac{\text{number of favorable outcomes}}{\text{total number of possible outcomes}}$$

$$= \frac{2}{6} \longleftarrow \text{Two parts of the circle are red.}$$

$$= \frac{1}{3}$$

Answer the following questions. Write answers in simplest form.

1. What is the probability of the arrow

    a. landing on 1? _____

    b. landing on 2? _____

    c. landing on 3? _____

    d. landing on 4? _____

    e. landing on 5? _____

    f. landing on 6? _____

    g. landing on 7? _____

    h. Add up the probabilities. What is the sum? _____

2. Flip a coin 10 times. What is the probability of landing heads up? _____
   of landing tails up? _____

3. Flip a coin 20 times. What is the probability of landing heads up? _____
   of landing tails up? _____

Lesson 11.5   Problem Solving

Solve each problem. Write answers in simplest form.

1. Jorge bought 20 of the 200 raffle tickets that were sold. There will be only 1 winning ticket. What is the probability that Jorge has a winning ticket?

    Jorge has a _____ chance of having a winning ticket.

2. Twenty-five people are selecting positions for a soccer game. Two will be goalies, 20 will be field players, and 3 will be referees. Each of the 25 people will select one of the 3 positions from a hat. What are the chances that each person will be a goalie? a field player? a referee?

    The chances of being chosen as a goalie are _____.

    The chances of being chosen as a field player

    are _____.

    The chances of being chosen as a referee are _____.

3. A bag of marbles contains 10 black, 5 green, and 15 yellow marbles. What is the probability of picking a black marble? a green marble? a yellow marble?

    The probability of picking a black marble is _____.

    The probability of picking a green marble is _____.

    The probability of picking a yellow marble is _____.

4. Paul has 25 pennies, 20 nickels, and 15 dimes in a box. If he picks one coin without looking, what are the chances that he will pick a penny? a nickel? a dime?

    There is a _____ chance he will pick a penny.

    There is a _____ chance he will pick a nickel.

    There is a _____ chance he will pick a dime.

1.

2.

3.

4.

Check What You Learned

Graphs and Probability

Interpret the bar graph. Answer each question.

1. What does the x axis represent?

   _____

2. What does the y axis represent?

   _____

3. How many students get 7 hours of sleep each night? _____

4. How many more students said they get 7 hours than 6 hours? _____

5. How many students were surveyed? _____

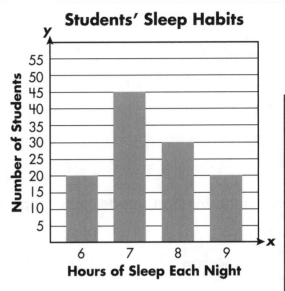

Students' Sleep Habits

Interpret the line graph. Answer each question.

6. What is the average weight of a two-year-old boy? _____

7. What is the average weight of a nine-year-old boy? _____

8. How many years does it take a boy to increase from 30 lb. to 50 lb.?

   _____

9. Which age shows the smallest weight gain? _____

10. Which age shows the greatest increase in weight? _____

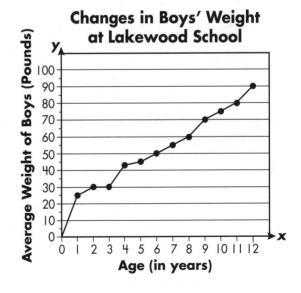

Changes in Boys' Weight at Lakewood School

Check What You Learned

Graphs and Probability

Find the mean of each set of numbers.

11. 7, 4, 9, 3, 12 _____

12. 64, 62, 71, 59, 72, 66, 54 _____

13. 18, 13, 25, 29, 16, 25 _____

14. 5 in., 12 in., 17 in., 18 in., 7 in., 15 in., 10 in. _____

15. $38, $49, $39, $55, $39 _____

16. 1472, 1341, 1389, 1402 _____

Find the median, mode, and range of each data set.

17. 12, 9, 18, 15, 9, 11, 13

median _____   mode _____   range _____

18. 15, 19, 17, 26, 24, 15, 24, 19, 19, 27, 21

median _____   mode _____   range _____

19. 68, 74, 68, 71, 75, 76, 69, 74, 68

median _____   mode _____   range _____

20. $180, $190, $183, $177, $177, $186, $179

median _____   mode _____   range _____

SHOW YOUR WORK

Solve the problem.

21. Kelly bought 8 apples, 3 pears, and 13 oranges and brought them home in a grocery bag. If she picks one from the bag without looking, what is the probability of choosing an apple? a pear? an orange?

The chances of choosing an apple are _____.

The chances of choosing a pear are _____.

The chances of choosing an orange are? _____.

21.

Check What You Know

Geometry

Label the following as line, line segment, or ray.

a   b

1. _____   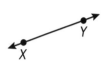 _____

_____

2. _____    _____

_____   _____

Identify each pair of lines as parallel, perpendicular, or intersecting.

3.  _____   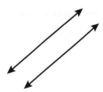 _____

4.  _____   _____

Name each angle. Label as acute, obtuse, or right.

5. _____   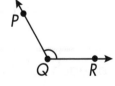 _____

_____   _____

6. 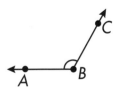 _____   _____

_____   _____

NAME _Victoria Kwei_

Check What You Know

Geometry

Use a protractor to measure the following angles.

	a		b	
7.		degrees _30°_		degrees _135°_

Identify the following quadrilaterals. Write the number that refers to the correct figure.

8. rhombus ___1___

9. kite ___4___

10. trapezoid ___3___

11. parallelogram ___2___

Identify the following polygons.

	a	Type	b	Type
12.		_rectangle_		_triangle_
13.		_square_		_hexagon_

Describe the surfaces of each solid figure.

14. 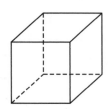 _square_   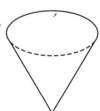 _circle_

Lesson 12.1 Points, Lines, Rays, and Angles

A

A **point** can be represented by a dot. The point on the left is called point A.

A **line** passes through two points. The line AB (denoted $\overleftrightarrow{AB}$) is the line that passes through points A and B. Also, $\overleftrightarrow{AB} = \overleftrightarrow{BA}$.

A **line segment** starts at a point A and ends at a point B, and includes all points in between. The line segment AB (denoted $\overline{AB}$) is the same as $\overline{BA}$.

A **ray** is a straight line that begins at an endpoint (A) and goes on forever in a certain direction. The ray at left is written as $\overrightarrow{AB}$.

Identify the following as point, line, line segment, or ray. Then, name each figure.

	a		b	

1.

line segment
$\overline{PQ}$

line
$\overleftrightarrow{BA}$

2.

ray
$\overrightarrow{RS}$

• R

point
point R

3.

line
$\overleftrightarrow{GH}$

ray
$\overrightarrow{PQ}$

Lesson 12.1 Points, Lines, Rays, and Angles

The **angle** ABC (denoted ∠ABC) is made of ray BA ($\overrightarrow{BA}$) and ray BC ($\overrightarrow{BC}$). The point where the two rays intersect is called the **vertex**. The vertex of ∠ABC is point B.

An angle can be measured using a **protractor**. A protractor measures angles that range from 0° to 180°.

Identify the rays and vertex of each angle. Name the angle.

	a		b	

1.

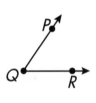

rays: $\overrightarrow{QP}$
$\overrightarrow{QR}$
vertex: Q
angle: acute

rays: $\overrightarrow{ED}$
$\overrightarrow{EF}$
vertex: E
angle: right

2.

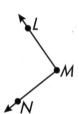

rays: $\overrightarrow{LM}$
$\overrightarrow{MN}$
vertex: M
angle: right

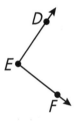

rays: $\overrightarrow{BA}$
$\overrightarrow{BC}$
vertex: B
angle: right

3.

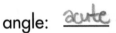

rays: $\overrightarrow{21}$
$\overrightarrow{23}$
vertex: 2
angle: right

rays: $\overrightarrow{SR}$
$\overrightarrow{ST}$
vertex: S
angle: acute

4.

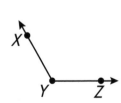

rays: $\overrightarrow{YX}$
$\overrightarrow{YZ}$
vertex: Y
angle: obtuse

rays: $\overrightarrow{78}$
$\overrightarrow{76}$
vertex: 7
angle: obtuse

Lesson 12.2 Parallel and Perpendicular Lines

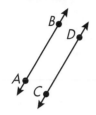 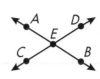 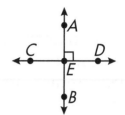

Lines like $\overleftrightarrow{AB}$ and $\overleftrightarrow{CD}$ are called **parallel lines** since they have no points in common. $\overleftrightarrow{AB}$ and $\overleftrightarrow{CD}$ will never intersect.

Lines like $\overleftrightarrow{AB}$ and $\overleftrightarrow{CD}$ are called **intersecting lines**. They have one point in common, point E. $\overleftrightarrow{AB}$ intersects $\overleftrightarrow{CD}$ at point E.

Lines like $\overleftrightarrow{AB}$ and $\overleftrightarrow{CD}$ are called **perpendicular lines**. They form a right angle, shown by the symbol ⌐ in the angle.

Identify each pair of lines as parallel, intersecting, or perpendicular.

	a		**b**	
	Type of Lines		Type of Lines	

1.
_____ _____

2.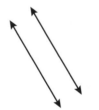
_____ 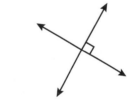 _____

3.
_____  _____

4.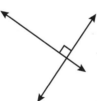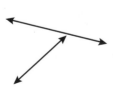
_____  _____

Lesson 12.3 Measuring Angles

A **protractor** is used to measure an angle. The angle is measured in degrees.

A **right angle** measures exactly 90°.

An **acute angle** measures less than 90°.

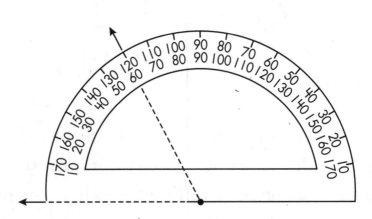

An **obtuse angle** measures greater than 90° but less than 180°.

Identify each angle as right, acute, or obtuse.

	a	Type of Angle	b	Type of Angle

1.   _____   _____

2.   _____ _____

3.   _____  _____

Lesson 12.3   Measuring Angles

Use a protractor to measure each angle.

                      a   **b**

1.

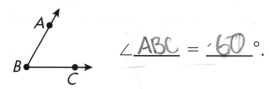   ∠ABC = 60 °.   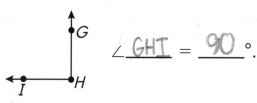   ∠GHI = 90 °.

2.

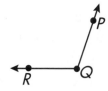   ∠PQR = 110 °.      ∠XYZ = 170 °.

3.

   ∠123 = 90 °.   ∠ABC = 30 °.

Find the measure of each angle of the given triangle. Label each angle as right, acute, or obtuse.

4.

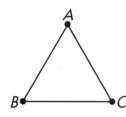

∠ABC = 60 °.
It is acute.
∠BCA = 60 °.
It is acute.
∠BAC = 60 °.
It is acute.

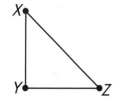

∠XYZ = 90 °.
It is right.
∠YZX = 45 °.
It is acute.
∠ZXY = 45 °.
It is acute.

Lesson 12.4   Quadrilaterals

A **quadrilateral** is a polygon with four sides. Some examples are square, rectangle, parallelogram, rhombus, kite, and trapezoid.

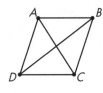 **parallelogram**
$\angle DAB = \angle BCD$,
$\angle ADC = \angle CBA$,
$\overline{AB} = \overline{DC}$, $\overline{AD} = \overline{BC}$.
$\overline{AC}$ bisects $\overline{BD}$. $\overline{BD}$ bisects $\overline{AC}$. $\triangle ADC$ is congruent to $\triangle CBA$.

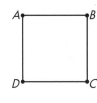 A **square** is a rectangle with 4 sides of same length.
$\overline{AB} = \overline{BC} = \overline{CD} = \overline{DA}$
and all angles equal
$\angle ADC = \angle DCB = \angle CBA = \angle BAD = 90°$

 A **rectangle** is a parallelogram with four right angles. Opposite sides are equal. $\overline{AB} = \overline{DC}$, $\overline{AD} = \overline{BC}$, $\angle BAD = \angle ABC = \angle BCD = \angle CDA = 90°$.

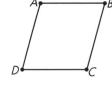 A **rhombus** is a parallelogram with all four sides the same length. Opposite angles are the same measure.

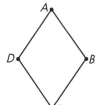 A **kite** has 2 pairs of adjacent sides that are congruent.

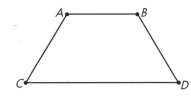 A **trapezoid** has just 2 sides that are parallel.

Identify each of the quadrilaterals.

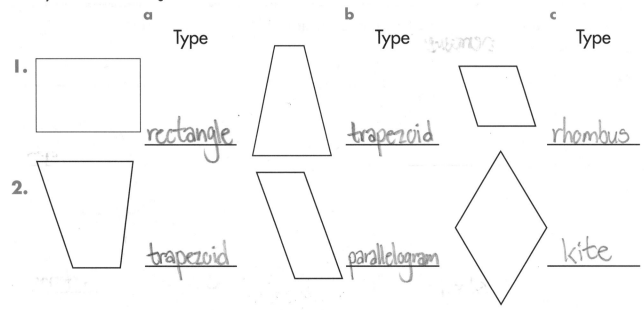

	a Type	**b** Type	**c** Type
1.	rectangle	trapezoid	rhombus
2.	trapezoid	parallelogram	kite

Lesson 12.5 Polygons

A **polygon** is a closed shape that is formed by three or more sides. The name of a polygon is given by the number of sides the shape has.

 A triangle has 3 sides.

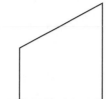 A quadrilateral has 4 sides.

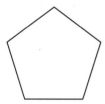 A pentagon has 5 sides.

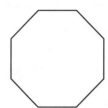 A hexagon has 6 sides.

 A heptagon has 7 sides.

 An octagon has 8 sides.

Identify each of the following polygons.

	a	b	c
	Type	Type	Type

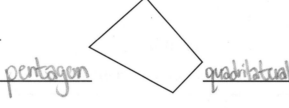

1.   pentagon   quadrilateral   triangle

2.   pentagon   triangle    hexagon

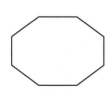
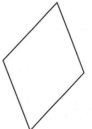

3.   octagon   quadrilateral   heptagon

Lesson 12.6 Solid Figures

Solid figures are three-dimensional figures. They are named for the types of surfaces they have. These surfaces may be flat, curved, or both.

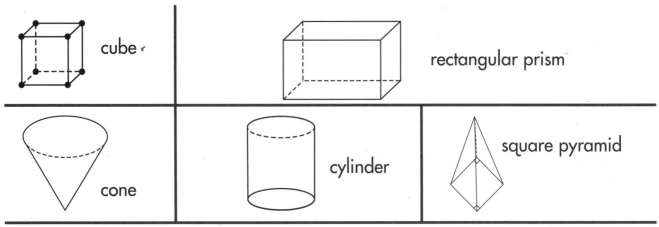

cube

rectangular prism

cone

cylinder

square pyramid

Solid figures have faces, edges, and vertices.

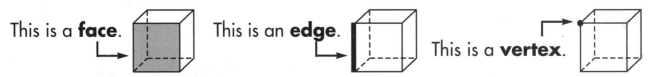

This is a **face**.

This is an **edge**.

This is a **vertex**.

Answer the following questions.

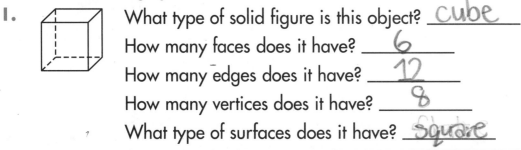

1. What type of solid figure is this object? __cube__
   How many faces does it have? __6__
   How many edges does it have? __12__
   How many vertices does it have? __8__
   What type of surfaces does it have? __square__

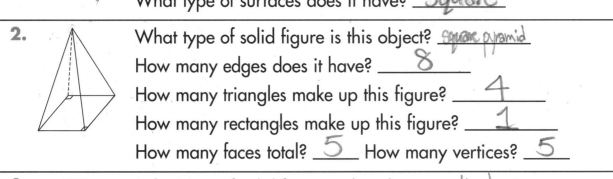

2. What type of solid figure is this object? __square pyramid__
   How many edges does it have? __8__
   How many triangles make up this figure? __4__
   How many rectangles make up this figure? __1__
   How many faces total? __5__ How many vertices? __5__

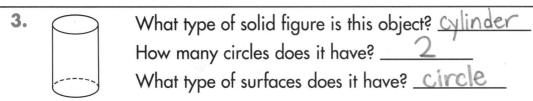

3. What type of solid figure is this object? __cylinder__
   How many circles does it have? __2__
   What type of surfaces does it have? __circle__

Check What You Learned

Geometry

Label the following as line, line segment, or ray. Name each figure.

a   b

1.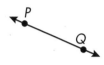

_____   _____

2.

_____   _____

Identify each pair of lines as parallel, perpendicular, or intersecting.

3.

_____   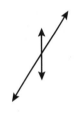 _____

4.

_____   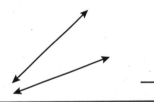 _____

Name each angle. Label as acute, obtuse, or right.

5.

_____   _____

6.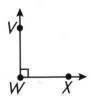

_____    _____

Check What You Learned

Geometry

Use a protractor to measure each angle.

a b

7. _____  _____

Identify the following quadrilaterals.

Type Type

8. 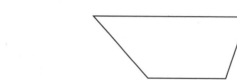 _____ _____

9. _____ _____

Match each figure with the number of the polygon.

10. triangle _____

11. pentagon _____

12. heptagon _____

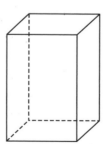

Complete the information for each solid figure.

13.

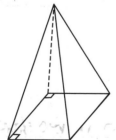

faces: _____

edges: _____

vertices: _____

type: _____

faces: _____

edges: _____

vertices: _____

type: _____

NAME Victoria Kwei

 Check What You Know

Preparing for Algebra

Find the next three terms of the repeating pattern.

a   b

1. 8, 10, 12, 14, _16_ , _18_ , _20_   22, 29, 36, 43, _50_ , _57_ , _64_

2. 100, 97, 94, 91, 88, _85_ , _82_ , _79_   65, 55, 45, 35, _25_ , _15_ , _5_

Find the next three terms of the ascending or descending pattern.

3. 1, 2, 4, 7, 11, _16_ , _22_ , _29_   5, 10, 20, 35, 55, _80_ , _110_ , _145_

4. 60, 58, 54, 48, 40, _30_ , _18_ , _4_   0, 4, 8, 12, 16, _20_ , _24_ , _28_

5. 2, 4, 8, 16, 32, _64_ , _128_ , _256_   729, 243, 81, _27_ , _9_ , _3_

Name the variable in each expression.

6.   a pile of leaves plus six extra   the height of a tree plus 4 feet

      #of leaves in pile   _the height of a tree_

7. x minus forty-three   videos in a video store multiplied by
                                                four video stores

      _____ $\times$ _____   _#of videos in video store_

Spectrum Math
Grade 5

NAME Victoria Kwei

 Check What You Know

Preparing for Algebra

Rewrite each variable expression.

	a	b
8.	a hike plus 50 yards	a pile of leaves plus 15 more
	$x + 50$	$x + 15$
9.	forty divided by p	number of classrooms in a school multiplied by 20 students in each class
	$40 \div p$	$x \times 20$
10.	some bags of candy minus 13 pieces	twenty-two multiplied by t
	$x - 13$	$22 \times t$

Write each equation as an open sentence.

11. $t + 33 = 72$ $14 + x = 30$

t plus 33 equals 72.   14 plus x equals 30.

12. $y - 4 = 23$ $6 \times y = 12$

y minus 4 equals 23.   6 times y equals 12.

SHOW YOUR WORK

Solve each problem.

13. The zookeeper fed 120 pounds of meat to the lions on Saturday. After being fed on Sunday, the lions had eaten a total of 260 pounds. How many pounds of meat were the lions given on Sunday? Write an equation to express this problem.

140; 120 + x = 260

13.
$$\begin{array}{r} 260 \\ -120 \\ \hline 140 \end{array}$$

14. A group of 9 friends went to the store and bought 36 notebooks for school. Each friend bought the same number of notebooks. How many notebooks did each friend buy? Write an equation to express this problem.

4; 9 × x = 36

14.
$$9\overline{)36} \quad 4$$

Lesson 13.1   Number Patterns

To determine the pattern in a set of numbers, look at the relationship between each pair of consecutive numbers. To find this relationship, subtract one number from the next number in the pattern.

Find the next three numbers in the following pattern.

$$3, 7, 11, 15, 19, \underline{\quad}, \underline{\quad}, \underline{\quad}$$

$$+4 \quad +4 \quad +4 \quad +4$$

This is a repeating pattern. Each number in the pattern is found by adding 4 to the preceding number.

$3 + 4 = 7$

$7 + 4 = 11$

$11 + 4 = 15$ The next three numbers in the pattern are 23, 27, 31.

$15 + 4 = 19$

$19 + 4 = 23$

In this set of numbers, the difference between consecutive numbers increases by one to get the next number in the pattern. This is an example of a *growing* or *ascending* pattern.

$$2, 3, 4, 8, 12$$

$$+1 \quad +2 \quad +3 \quad +4$$

Find the numbers to complete each pattern.

	a		b

1. 1, 4, 7, 10, 13, 16, ___ , ___ , ___   10, 15, 20, 25, ___ , ___ , ___

2. 10, 9, 8, 7, ___ , ___ , ___   60, 54, 48, 42, 36, ___ , ___ , ___

3. 12, 13, 15, 18, 22, ___ , ___ , ___   140, 142, 144, 146, ___ , ___ , ___

4. 6, 9, 15, 24, 39, ___ , ___ , ___   108, 99, 90, 81, ___ , ___ , ___

5. 2, 4, 8, 14, 22, 32, ___ , ___ , ___   1, 3, 6, 9, 12, 15, 18, ___ , ___ , ___

NAME _____

Lesson 13.2 Variable Expressions

A **variable** is an unknown quantity that represents any one of a set of numbers or other objects.

A **variable expression** is a verbal statement with a numerical value and an unknown quantity.

For example:

a pizza plus 3 extra pieces

This expression can be written as shown at the right.

The variable is the number of pizzas, x.

_____$x + 3$_____.

Write the variable in each expression. Then rewrite the expression.

a	b
1. a few weeks plus two extra days	three cherries and some extras
variable: number of weeks	variable: _____
expression: $x + 2$	expression: _____
2. eight more than x	a field of corn plus 10 extra ears
variable: _____	variable: _____
expression: _____	expression: _____
3. a number y minus 32	five cookies plus a bag of cookies
variable: _____	variable: _____
expression: _____	expression: _____
4. eight inches added to a fence	a number 61 plus p
variable: _____	variable: _____
expression: _____	expression: _____
5. four gardens of plants	a number y multiplied by 6
variable: _____	variable: _____
expression: _____	expression: _____
6. a number p divided by 9	52 cards in each deck
variable: _____	variable: _____
expression: _____	expression: _____

Lesson 13.3 Open Sentences

An **open sentence** is a math sentence containing a variable (y) and an equals sign.

$y + 6 = 14$ can be written as *y plus 6 equals 14.*

Ten times a number is 20 can be written as $10 \times y = 20$.

A sentence that has an equals sign is called an **equation**.

Write each expression as an open sentence.

	a	b
1.	$x + 3 = 7$	$x + 9 = 12$
	x plus three equals seven.	_____
2.	$25 + r = 41$	$r - 11 = 28$
	_____	_____
3.	$58 - x = 17$	$10 \times k = 90$
	_____	_____
4.	$18 - y = 10$	$4 \times t = 64$
	_____	_____
5.	$12 \div x = 3$	$100 \div p = 25$
	_____	_____

Write an equation for each sentence.

6. Eight divided by 2 is a number.

Twelve plus a number is 14.

7. A number times 7 is 14.

A number less 14 is 6.

Lesson 13.4 Problem Solving

Solve each problem.

1. The last four digits of Maureen's phone number are 3487. The last four digits of Steven's phone number are 3489. The last four digits of Jennifer's phone number are 3491. If the last four digits of Michael's phone number is the next term in this pattern, what are they?

   The last four digits of Michael's phone number are

   _____.

1.

2. The distance between consecutive stoplights forms a repeating pattern. The first stoplight is 400 meters from the second. The second stoplight is 350 meters from the third and the third stoplight is 300 meters from the fourth. How far is the fourth stop light from the fifth? How far is the fifth stop light from the sixth?

   The fourth stoplight is _____ meters from the fifth.

   The fifth stoplight is _____ meters from the sixth.

2.

3. There are four pieces of string with lengths that form a repeating pattern. The difference between consecutive lengths is 3. The first piece of string is 4 inches long. How long are the remaining three pieces?

   The second piece of string is _____ inches long.

   The third piece of string is _____ inches long.

   The fourth piece of string is _____ inches long.

4. Barbara has 19 apples. She needs a total of 30 apples to give her mother. How many more apples does Barbara need? Write an equation to express this problem.

   _____

3.

4.

Check What You Learned

Preparing for Algebra

Find the next three terms of each pattern.

	a		b

1. 1, 10, 19, 28, 37, ___ , ___ , ___   84, 72, 60, 48, ___ , ___ , ___

2. 6241, 6243, 6247, 6255, ___ , ___ , ___   8, 12, 16, 20, ___ , ___ , ___

3. 2, 3, 5, 8, 12, 17, 23, ___ , ___ , ___   1024, 512, 256, 128, ___ , ___ , ___

Name the variable in each expression.

4. number of lightbulbs in a house
    plus 12 light bulbs

    _____

    y minus three

    _____

5. a load of clothes multiplied by
    two loads of laundry

    _____

    number of eggs in a carton
    divided by three

    _____

Rewrite each variable expression.

6. an order of fries plus 13 fries

    _____

    number of chairs in a classroom
    plus 32 chairs

    _____

7. an orchard of apples
    minus 55 apples

    _____

    number of people at an amusement
    park multiplied by three parks

    _____

8. a pile of books multiplied by
    six piles

    _____

    a number of kilometers
    divided by three trails

    _____

Check What You Learned

Preparing for Algebra

Write each expression as an open sentence.

	a	b
9.	$7 + x = 21$	$50 - y = 35$
10.	$s \times 12 = 84$	$x - 20 = 13$
11.	$14 \div y = 2$	$36 \div r = 4$
12.	$17 + x = 35$	$38 - t = 16$

SHOW YOUR WORK

Solve each problem.

13. Santo found 2 pennies on Sunday, 4 pennies on Monday, 8 pennies on Tuesday, and 16 pennies on Wednesday. If this pattern continues, how many pennies will he find on Thursday and Friday?

He will find _____ pennies on Thursday.

He will find _____ pennies on Friday.

14. Paul can work 49 hours next week. He expects to spend 7 hours on each job. How many jobs does he have? Write an equation to express this problem.

_____

15. Winona had 32 ounces of flour. She used some for baking and now has only 24 ounces. How much flour did Winona use? Write an equation to express this problem.

_____

13.

14.   **15.**

Final Test   Chapters 1–13

Add or subtract.

	a	b	c	d
1.	28 +97	479 +364	2417 +3299	81935 +14367
2.	53 −28	291 − 28	4821 − 946	39217 − 3689
3.	421663 +312743	418 364 +1291	32010 41722 9264 + 1717	561823 − 64217

Multiply or divide.

	a	b	c	d
4.	18 × 7	32 ×17	149 × 6	582 × 27
5.	3)109	4)4364	24)3218	52)72714
6.	82041 × 6	37655 × 12	9274 × 216	36944 × 50

Spectrum Math
Grade 5

Final Test
Chapters 1–13
159

CHAPTERS 1–9 FINAL TEST

Final Test Chapters 1–13

Add or subtract. Write answers in simplest form.

	a	b	c	d
7.	$\dfrac{7}{12}$ $+\dfrac{1}{10}$	$\dfrac{2}{5}$ $+\dfrac{4}{5}$	$8\dfrac{9}{10}$ $+\dfrac{7}{10}$	$2\dfrac{1}{2}$ $+3\dfrac{6}{7}$
8.	$\dfrac{5}{8}$ $-\dfrac{1}{8}$	$\dfrac{5}{6}$ $+\dfrac{8}{9}$	6 $-\dfrac{4}{7}$	$7\dfrac{1}{4}$ $-3\dfrac{1}{3}$

Multiply or divide. Write answers in simplest form.

9. $\dfrac{1}{2} \times \dfrac{4}{7} =$ _____ $\dfrac{5}{8} \times \dfrac{3}{5} =$ _____ $\dfrac{7}{12} \times \dfrac{3}{8} =$ _____ $\dfrac{9}{10} \times \dfrac{10}{11} =$ _____

10. $\dfrac{3}{2} \div \dfrac{2}{3} =$ _____ $5 \div 7\dfrac{1}{2} =$ _____ $3\dfrac{1}{2} \div 2\dfrac{1}{4} =$ _____ $\dfrac{5}{7} \div \dfrac{20}{21} =$ _____

11. $4 \times 1\dfrac{2}{3} =$ _____ $2\dfrac{1}{6} \times 7\dfrac{4}{5} =$ _____ $4\dfrac{1}{5} \times 3 =$ _____ $5\dfrac{1}{7} \times 1\dfrac{5}{9} =$ _____

Final Test Chapters 1-13

Complete the following.

| a | b | c |

12. 20 mm = _____ cm   30 m = _____ cm   21 km = _____ m

13. 17 kL = _____ L   18,000 mL = _____ L   2 kL 972 L = _____ L

Find the perimeter of each figure.

14.

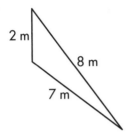

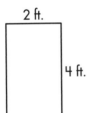

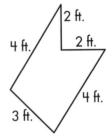

perimeter = _____ m   perimeter = _____ yd.   perimeter = _____ ft.

Find the area of each rectangle.

15.

2 ft.

4 ft.

10 in.

3 in.

5 cm

5 cm

area = _____ sq. ft.   area = _____ sq. in.   area = _____ sq. cm

Find the volume of each rectangular solid.

16.

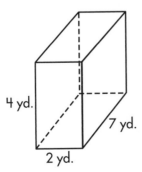

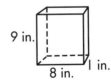

_____ cubic yd.   _____ cubic ft.   _____ cubic in.

Spectrum Math
Grade 5

Final Test
Chapters 1-13
161

CHAPTERS 1-9 FINAL TEST

Final Test Chapters 1–13

Match each figure to its name.

17. ray _____

18. perpendicular lines _____

19. acute angle _____

20. parallel lines _____

21. line _____

22. obtuse angle _____

23. line segment _____

24. point _____

25. right angle _____

26. intersecting lines _____

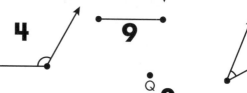

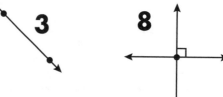
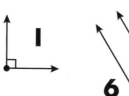

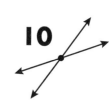

Find the mean, median, mode, and range of each data set.

27. 2, 4, 2, 6, 7, 6, 2, 3, 7 | 12, 17, 12, 29, 26, 25, 12 | $74, $65, $65, $75, $71

mean: _____	mean: _____	mean: _____
median: _____	median: _____	median: _____
mode: _____	mode: _____	mode: _____
range: _____	range: _____	range: _____

Identify each of the following polygons.

28.

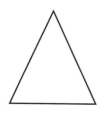
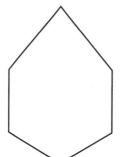
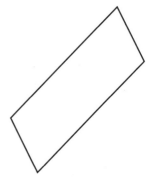

_____   _____   _____

Spectrum Math
Grade 5
162

CHAPTERS 1–9 FINAL TEST

Final Test
Chapters 1–13

Scoring Record for Posttests, Mid-Test, and Final Test

Chapter Posttest	Your Score	Performance			
		Excellent	Very Good	Fair	Needs Improvement
1	____ of 40	38–40	33–37	25–32	24 or fewer
2	____ of 25	24–25	21–23	16–20	15 or fewer
3	____ of 28	27–28	23–26	18–22	17 or fewer
4	____ of 39	37–39	32–36	24–31	23 or fewer
5	____ of 25	24–25	21–23	16–20	15 or fewer
6	____ of 25	24–25	21–23	16–20	15 or fewer
7	____ of 24	23–24	20–22	15–19	14 or fewer
8	____ of 26	25–26	21–24	17–20	16 or fewer
9	____ of 31	30–31	26–29	20–25	19 or fewer
10	____ of 24	23–24	20–22	15–19	14 or fewer
11	____ of 31	30–31	26–29	20–25	19 or fewer
12	____ of 37	35–37	31–34	23–30	22 or fewer
13	____ of 28	27–28	23–26	18–22	17 or fewer
Mid-Test	____ of 103	97–103	83–96	63–82	62 or fewer
Final Test	____ of 84	79–84	68–78	51–67	50 or fewer

Record your test score in the Your Score column. See where your score falls in the Performance columns. Your score is based on the total number of required responses. If your score is fair or needs improvement, review the chapter material.

Grade 5 Answers

Chapter 1

Pretest, page 1

	a	b	c	d	e
1.	63	107	84	102	140
2.	933	1205	802	1503	11352
3.	5520	7790	37733	82981	116737
4.	1450	8364	10312	35585	162339
5.	36	25	28	36	17
6.	189	559	430	168	418
7.	5342	7755	1777	5898	5253
8.	14171	22735	76228	26707	41257

Pretest, page 2

9. Add; 39   10. Add; 86   11. Add; 256
12. Subtract; 29   13. Subtract; 4749

Lesson 1.1, page 3

	a	b	c	d	e	f
1.	46	71	55	126	110	134
2.	129	109	70	96	130	123
3.	99	49	88	75	104	57
4.	31	63	25	41	26	59
5.	15	18	46	28	57	96
6.	38	54	188	74	377	623

Lesson 1.2, page 4

	a	b	c	d	e	f
1.	997	689	793	978	869	568
2.	893	401	985	557	914	1500
3.	1562	1142	1381	1122	1841	1703
4.	134	158	508	679	334	392
5.	442	227	385	4335	4536	2489
6.	985	6185	6976	2834	4183	1548
7.	2313	4847	7864	5987	8286	8629

Lesson 1.3, page 5

	a	b	c	d	e
1.	7987	10495	11759	49830	139021
2.	2302	8123	319	43582	9026
3.	55319	134240	114461	45661	393273
4.	28334	17777	31545	258886	695976
5.	675702	981402	319994	406616	1460016
6.	776367	312076	95708	445676	768849

Lesson 1.4, page 6

1. Add; 42   2. Add; 227   3. Subtract; 8,017
4. Subtract; 685   5. Subtract; 134

Lesson 1.5, page 7

	a	b	c	d	e
1.	964	1943	2444	1639	8206
2.	1906	7155	20414	68165	329128
3.	2153	7366	70287	88247	853367
5.	3673	13322	83542	106448	925436

Lesson 1.6, page 8

	a	b	c	d	e
1.	186	140	1324	854	6362
2.	9344	11602	49539	54331	612215
3.	1580	9080	39815	88824	897421
4.	106237	799152	2001	13755	136659
5.	26	39	34	16	283
6.	107	638	485	4925	5127
7.	1717	4781	378	73677	35477
8.	41818	37567	633228	88983	505108

Lesson 1.7, page 9

	a	b	c	d
1.	6000	9000	5000	80000
2.	3000	33000	40000	60000
3.	70000	120000	70000	500000
4.	10000	170000	500000	400000
5.	900000	16000	160000	1130000

Lesson 1.8, page 10

1. 200   2. 90,000   3. 12,000   4. 900   5. 800

Posttest, page 11

	a	b	c	d	e
1.	83	80	1347	500	1100
2.	31	7	367	486	774
3.	791	1372	6201	5911	8149
4.	679	2011	6619	7979	1034
5.	13561	49992	62073	151220	85718
6.	42506	70912	83747	633069	227935
7.	39031	541168	1621	12099	106457

Posttest, page 12

8. Add; 10,265   9. Subtract; 613
10. Add; 13,899   11. Subtract; 68   12. Add; 19,271

Chapter 2

Pretest, page 13

	a	b	c	d
1.	336	192	1175	6632
2.	6292	22206	1155	6768
3.	1715	8360	26112	22080
4.	141128	83456	71154	262578
5.	78320	2168280	2241194	1627838

Grade 5 Answers

Pretest, page 14
6. 8 **7.** 66 **8.** 17,918 **9.** 30,444 **10.** 70,560

Lesson 2.1, page 15
	a	b	c	d	e	f
1.	18	16	28	198	102	294
2.	444	306	168	163	1268	1325
3.	3344	5016	704	511	585	174
4.	130	672	276	1032	5888	5694
5.	3525	1022	5652	74	97	208
6.	4580	552	1419	2848	2300	1758

Lesson 2.2, page 16
	a	b	c	d	e	f
1.	1806	900	1456	3276	1232	273
2.	2088	3348	3072	846	2607	2835
3.	1378	2886	3564	30272	18832	18375
4.	48604	24738	17112	51402	15836	20210
5.	29931	11205	29848	29538	45818	52972

Lesson 2.3, page 17
1. 32; 6; 192 **2.** 173; 4; 692 **3.** 24; 432
4. 47; 24; 1,128 **5.** 23; 26; 598

Lesson 2.4, page 18
	a	b	c	d	e
1.	13815	43428	12884	69072	43518
2.	18912	35658	3708	31638	13368
3.	22578	18856	104300	237318	118449
4.	339008	96025	370392	253980	585488
5.	96174	402354	159360	659736	239456

Lesson 2.5, page 19
	a	b	c	d
1.	114933	96768	197508	263900
2.	304263	327267	72352	163688
3.	346426	132890	713728	3419136
4.	418026	1128336	2701656	2142778
5.	2667390	2470292	2128560	585531

Lesson 2.6, page 20
	a	b	c	d
1.	130	171	846	5728
2.	15710	43897	50454	3600
3.	2356	8236	25830	19968
4.	88815	391196	431163	103487
5.	240096	181875	828736	2714900

Lesson 2.7, page 21
	a	b	c	d	e
1.	160	200	180	1500	2800
2.	300	8000	18000	42000	72000
3.	1800	2700	1200	6000	1600
4.	15000	28000	4000	8000	63000

5.	280000	150000	120000	320000	360000
6.	180000	400000	160000	280000	360000
7.	3000000	1500000	7000000	8100000	2800000

Lesson 2.8, page 22
1. 18,612 **2.** 999 **3.** 1,498 **4.** 91,785
5. 173,712 **6.** 48,792

Posttest, page 23
	a	b	c	d
1.	315	7758	1640	14856
2.	325	1888	26040	30118
3.	23856	532344	69056	447714
4.	118932	247038	147875	234250
5.	1181808	5165904	1031415	2108986

Posttest, page 24
6. 1,792 **7.** 15,246 **8.** 70,966
9. 314,732 **10.** 770,660

Chapter 3

Pretest, page 25
	a	b	c	d
1.	254	60r3	293	2073r2
2.	4261	4943r1	7	3
3.	3r11	2r11	3	18
4.	27r23	14r5	135	64r88
5.	62r13	88r51	2368	348r29

Pretest, page 26
6. 49 **7.** 209 **8.** 81 **9.** 152; 6
10. 25 **11.** 11; 10

Lesson 3.1, page 27
	a	b	c	d	e	f
1.	3	2	2	2	7	9
2.	0	5	2	3	18	1
3.	5	4	2	1	2	3
4.	5	4	5	9	11	7
5.	3	3	9	5	9	5
6.	7	1	6	3	7	6
7.	9	9	8	8	6	2
8.	6	8	4	4	5	5
9.	4	7	9	6	7	3
10.	2	4	4	6	8	7

Lesson 3.2, page 28
	a	b	c	d	e
1.	10r2	8r3	8r3	8r1	9r1
2.	16r2	12r5	24r3	17	6r2
3.	22	41r5	212r1	151r2	72
4.	437r1	76r5	79r7	46r1	143

Grade 5 Answers

Lesson 3.3, page 29

	a	b	c	d
1.	216r2	154r1	60r7	117
2.	70r6	142	203r5	1248r2
3.	1700r3	699r1	791r2	1158r1

Lesson 3.4, page 30

	a	b	c	d
1.	5	5	25	21
2.	7	40	60	110
3.	40	280	300	1400
4.	300	1800	400	1500

Lesson 3.5, page 31

	a	b	c	d
1.	2r2	5r7	2	2r11
2.	3r15	3r10	8r1	3r13
3.	1r7	3	3	2r7
4.	3	2r18	3r11	3r5

Lesson 3.6, page 32

	a	b	c	d
1.	11r11	17r27	8r76	6r16
2.	8	5	4r34	15r14
3.	9r18	16r7	21r13	11r22

Lesson 3.7, page 33

	a	b	c	d
1.	152r35	377	58r32	54r21
2.	50r29	60	109r20	168
3.	30	202r1	56r3	150r46

Lesson 3.8, page 34

	a	b	c	d
1.	1793r1	1631r30	340	1051r41
2.	901	2888r17	843r6	842r31

Lesson 3.9, page 35

	a	b	c	d
1.	931r2	849	12285	9052r4
2.	6r5	2r2	1r32	14r20
3.	17r36	3r12	20r27	69r60
4.	69r8	453r33	1272r23	1385r33

Lesson 3.10, page 36

1. 56; 784; 14   2. 18; 126; 7
3. 3,615; 15; 241   4. 618; 87; 7; 9

Posttest, page 37

	a	b	c	d
1.	357	2169	7264	25404r2
2.	6	2r10	2r23	3r4
3.	8	17r11	10r25	4r33
4.	28	49r43	177r39	46r46
5.	2648	339r29	3621r12	694r38

Posttest, page 38

6. 18 **7.** 223 **8.** 1,055 **9.** 7; 9
10. 133; 30 **11.** 642

Chapter 4

Pretest, page 39

	a	b	c
1.	prime	composite	composite
2.	composite	composite	composite
3.	2	25	18
4.	8	2	8
5.	2×3	3×7	$3 \times 2 \times 2$
6.	5×5	$2 \times 2 \times 2 \times 2 \times 2$	$2 \times 2 \times 11$
7.	$\frac{2}{3}$	$\frac{1}{3}$	$\frac{5}{8}$
8.	$\frac{3}{7}$	$\frac{5}{6}$	$\frac{8}{9}$
9.	$\frac{6}{7}$	$\frac{1}{2}$	$\frac{9}{10}$

Pretest, page 40

	a	b	c
10.	$1\frac{3}{7}$	$8\frac{1}{3}$	$2\frac{2}{7}$
11.	$1\frac{5}{18}$	$4\frac{2}{7}$	$2\frac{3}{4}$
12.	$\frac{11}{4}$	$\frac{62}{9}$	$\frac{107}{12}$
13.	$\frac{40}{9}$	$\frac{37}{7}$	$\frac{18}{5}$
14.	$5\frac{1}{2}$	$4\frac{2}{3}$	$9\frac{1}{4}$
15.	$9\frac{2}{5}$	$3\frac{2}{3}$	$3\frac{3}{4}$

Lesson 4.1, page 41

	a	b
1.	$\frac{2}{7}$	$\frac{3}{4}$
2.	$\frac{1}{9}$	$\frac{3}{5}$
3.	$\frac{7}{8}$	$\frac{9}{10}$
4.	seven-ninths	one-fourth
5.	three-tenths	five-sixths
6.	$\frac{1}{2}$	$\frac{1}{3}$
7.	$\frac{3}{8}$	$\frac{7}{12}$

Lesson 4.2, page 42

	a	b
1.	composite	composite
2.	prime	composite
3.	prime	prime
4.	composite	prime
5.	prime	composite
6.	composite	composite
7.	$2 \times 2 \times 2 \times 2 \times 2$	$2 \times 3 \times 13$
8.	2×37	$2 \times 3 \times 3$
9.	$2 \times 2 \times 2 \times 2 \times 2 \times 3$	5×11
10.	2×19	$2 \times 2 \times 2 \times 3$
11.	$3 \times 3 \times 3$	$3 \times 3 \times 7$
12.	3×17	$2 \times 2 \times 2 \times 11$

Lesson 4.3, page 43

	a	b
1.	14	9
2.	12	5
3.	18	7
4.	2	11
5.	26	4
6.	3	16
7.	5	9

Lesson 4.4, page 44

	a	b	c
1.	$\frac{1}{2}$	$\frac{1}{2}$	$\frac{1}{2}$
2.	$\frac{1}{4}$	$\frac{1}{3}$	$1\frac{5}{6}$
3.	$\frac{1}{5}$	$\frac{4}{5}$	$1\frac{1}{4}$
4.	$\frac{1}{2}$	$\frac{13}{14}$	$1\frac{1}{4}$
5.	$\frac{5}{7}$	$\frac{17}{25}$	$\frac{7}{9}$
6.	$\frac{11}{32}$	$\frac{7}{9}$	$\frac{1}{4}$

Lesson 4.5, page 45

	a	b	c
1.	$1\frac{2}{3}$	$1\frac{1}{6}$	$1\frac{4}{5}$
2.	$1\frac{1}{2}$	$1\frac{1}{3}$	$1\frac{3}{5}$
3.	$1\frac{2}{5}$	$1\frac{2}{7}$	$1\frac{1}{4}$
4.	$5\frac{1}{3}$	$12\frac{3}{4}$	$5\frac{4}{9}$
5.	$13\frac{1}{5}$	$27\frac{2}{3}$	$5\frac{3}{5}$
6.	$9\frac{2}{3}$	$5\frac{3}{7}$	$10\frac{2}{3}$

Lesson 4.6, page 46

	a	b	c	d	e
1.	$\frac{26}{3}$	$\frac{55}{8}$	$\frac{19}{2}$	$\frac{39}{7}$	$\frac{12}{7}$
2.	$\frac{115}{13}$	$\frac{29}{12}$	$\frac{53}{16}$	$\frac{17}{6}$	$6\frac{1}{8}$
3.	$2\frac{3}{4}$	$4\frac{1}{2}$	$8\frac{1}{3}$	$5\frac{1}{3}$	$3\frac{3}{4}$
4.	$4\frac{3}{5}$	$7\frac{1}{3}$	$2\frac{2}{5}$	$6\frac{2}{7}$	$8\frac{1}{4}$

Posttest, page 47

	a	b
1.	composite	prime
2.	prime	composite
3.	5	14
4.	2	16
5.	$2 \times 2 \times 2 \times 2 \times 2 \times 2$	3×17
6.	$\frac{2}{3}$	$\frac{1}{3}$
7.	$\frac{5}{8}$	$\frac{3}{7}$
8.	$\frac{5}{6}$	$\frac{8}{9}$
9.	$\frac{1}{2}$	$\frac{8}{9}$

Posttest, page 48

	a	b	c
10.	$5\frac{1}{2}$	$1\frac{1}{8}$	$2\frac{5}{6}$
11.	$2\frac{5}{9}$	$2\frac{1}{6}$	$1\frac{1}{12}$
12.	$4\frac{1}{2}$	$1\frac{5}{12}$	12
13.	$6\frac{1}{6}$	$5\frac{4}{9}$	$6\frac{1}{4}$
14.	$3\frac{3}{4}$	$9\frac{2}{3}$	$4\frac{1}{2}$
15.	$8\frac{2}{3}$	$3\frac{1}{2}$	$6\frac{1}{5}$
16.	$11\frac{1}{2}$	$1\frac{5}{7}$	$3\frac{1}{8}$

Chapter 5

Pretest, page 49

	a	b	c	d
1.	$\frac{7}{8}$	$\frac{6}{7}$	$\frac{1}{2}$	$\frac{7}{9}$
2.	$1\frac{3}{4}$	$1\frac{1}{20}$	$1\frac{1}{2}$	1
3.	$7\frac{3}{4}$	$11\frac{8}{9}$	$12\frac{5}{6}$	$17\frac{2}{3}$
4.	8	2	10	25
5.	8	42	66	28

Pretest, page 50

6. $4\frac{1}{3}$ 7. $8\frac{1}{2}$ 8. $1\frac{13}{20}$ 9. $7\frac{11}{14}$ 10. $3\frac{19}{24}$

Lesson 5.1, page 51

	a	b	c	d	e
1.	$\frac{2}{3}$	$\frac{3}{5}$	$\frac{7}{9}$	$\frac{6}{7}$	$\frac{1}{3}$
2.	$\frac{4}{5}$	$\frac{4}{7}$	$\frac{3}{4}$	$\frac{2}{5}$	$\frac{4}{5}$
3.	$\frac{1}{2}$	$\frac{2}{3}$	$\frac{9}{11}$	$\frac{5}{7}$	$\frac{1}{2}$
4.	$\frac{3}{4}$	$\frac{3}{5}$	$\frac{4}{5}$	$\frac{8}{11}$	$\frac{6}{7}$

Lesson 5.1, page 52

	a	b	c	d	e
1.	$1\frac{1}{2}$	1	$1\frac{3}{5}$	$1\frac{1}{6}$	$1\frac{2}{7}$
2.	$1\frac{2}{5}$	1	1	$1\frac{1}{4}$	$1\frac{1}{4}$
3.	$1\frac{3}{5}$	$1\frac{2}{7}$	$1\frac{3}{4}$	1	$1\frac{1}{3}$
4.	$1\frac{1}{4}$	$1\frac{2}{11}$	$1\frac{2}{3}$	1	$1\frac{1}{2}$

Lesson 5.2, page 53

	a	b	c	d	e
1.	9	15	$10\frac{1}{3}$	$7\frac{1}{5}$	$11\frac{10}{11}$
2.	$12\frac{1}{5}$	$9\frac{1}{2}$	$5\frac{1}{7}$	$15\frac{1}{2}$	$9\frac{4}{9}$
3.	$7\frac{7}{11}$	8	$12\frac{2}{3}$	$13\frac{3}{4}$	$8\frac{2}{7}$
4.	$10\frac{5}{6}$	$16\frac{4}{5}$	14	$8\frac{2}{3}$	$14\frac{4}{5}$

Lesson 5.3, page 54

1. $\frac{2}{3}$ 2. $1\frac{2}{5}$ 3. $2\frac{3}{4}$ 4. 4 5. 2 6. 3

Grade 5 Answers

Lesson 5.4, page 55

	a	b	c
1.	6	15	4
2.	4	8	21
3.	18	15	12
4.	21	8	20

Lesson 5.4, page 56

	a	b	c
1.	2	9	6
2.	12	6	35
3.	35	20	6
4.	27	24	25
5.	18	14	48

Lesson 5.5, page 57

	a	b	c	d	e
1.	$\frac{17}{20}$	$\frac{20}{21}$	$\frac{12}{35}$	$\frac{13}{24}$	$\frac{5}{6}$
2.	$\frac{61}{72}$	$1\frac{4}{21}$	$1\frac{4}{35}$	$1\frac{1}{30}$	$\frac{31}{56}$
3.	$\frac{13}{15}$	$1\frac{8}{63}$	$1\frac{1}{20}$	$1\frac{11}{40}$	$1\frac{47}{63}$

Lesson 5.5, page 58

	a	b	c	d	e
1.	$1\frac{1}{4}$	$\frac{7}{10}$	$1\frac{7}{12}$	$1\frac{1}{6}$	$\frac{3}{4}$
2.	$\frac{5}{8}$	$1\frac{2}{9}$	$1\frac{7}{24}$	$1\frac{1}{5}$	$1\frac{7}{12}$
3.	1	$1\frac{1}{24}$	$1\frac{21}{40}$	$1\frac{5}{36}$	$1\frac{13}{18}$

Lesson 5.6, page 59

	a	b	c	d
1.	$5\frac{9}{10}$	$7\frac{13}{15}$	$8\frac{1}{28}$	$7\frac{9}{20}$
2.	$9\frac{31}{42}$	$9\frac{13}{30}$	$10\frac{17}{24}$	$13\frac{13}{18}$
3.	$16\frac{11}{24}$	$14\frac{17}{21}$	$10\frac{61}{63}$	$9\frac{2}{15}$
4.	$14\frac{11}{30}$	$14\frac{31}{45}$	$12\frac{1}{24}$	$19\frac{43}{70}$

Lesson 5.7, page 60

1. $6\frac{2}{3}$ 2. $13\frac{4}{15}$ 3. $\frac{7}{12}$ 4. $5\frac{7}{8}$ 5. $6\frac{11}{21}$ 6. $10\frac{7}{12}$

Posttest, page 61

	a	b	c	d
1.	$\frac{5}{6}$	$\frac{5}{7}$	$\frac{8}{9}$	$1\frac{1}{8}$
2.	$1\frac{3}{11}$	$1\frac{7}{9}$	$1\frac{11}{60}$	$1\frac{3}{10}$
3.	$1\frac{11}{24}$	$1\frac{3}{35}$	13	$17\frac{4}{5}$
4.	35	72	32	21
5.	49	15	18	36

Posttest, page 62

6. 2   7. $7\frac{1}{6}$ 8. $5\frac{37}{45}$ 9. $13\frac{23}{30}$ 10. $9\frac{1}{6}$

Chapter 6

Pretest, page 63

	a	b	c	d
1.	$\frac{3}{4}$	$\frac{1}{9}$	$\frac{1}{2}$	$\frac{1}{2}$
2.	$\frac{1}{8}$	$\frac{2}{35}$	$\frac{22}{63}$	$5\frac{1}{3}$
3.	$1\frac{4}{5}$	$8\frac{1}{10}$	$\frac{1}{8}$	$3\frac{1}{3}$
4.	$4\frac{3}{5}$	$2\frac{1}{7}$	$4\frac{1}{12}$	$4\frac{5}{18}$

Pretest, page 64

5. $6\frac{3}{8}$ 6. $\frac{1}{3}$ 7. $\frac{25}{63}$ 8. $\frac{5}{9}$ 9. $\frac{3}{4}$

Lesson 6.1, page 65

	a	b	c	d
1.	$\frac{2}{7}$	$\frac{1}{2}$	$\frac{1}{2}$	$\frac{2}{5}$
2.	$\frac{2}{3}$	$\frac{2}{3}$	$\frac{1}{9}$	$\frac{5}{7}$
3.	$\frac{3}{5}$	$\frac{1}{2}$	$\frac{1}{6}$	$\frac{1}{4}$
4.	$\frac{1}{5}$	$\frac{1}{5}$	$\frac{1}{3}$	$\frac{4}{11}$

Lesson 6.2, page 66

	a	b	c	d	e
1.	$3\frac{1}{3}$	$5\frac{4}{5}$	$\frac{5}{7}$	$7\frac{1}{2}$	$3\frac{1}{6}$
2.	$6\frac{5}{6}$	$7\frac{2}{3}$	$1\frac{5}{8}$	$4\frac{2}{7}$	$8\frac{3}{5}$
3.	$4\frac{3}{10}$	$5\frac{1}{4}$	$2\frac{7}{11}$	$6\frac{3}{8}$	$7\frac{3}{4}$

Lesson 6.3, page 67

	a	b	c	d	e
1.	$2\frac{1}{2}$	$4\frac{1}{7}$	$6\frac{1}{4}$	$4\frac{2}{3}$	$3\frac{1}{4}$
2.	$3\frac{1}{3}$	$2\frac{3}{5}$	$2\frac{1}{5}$	2	$1\frac{5}{9}$
3.	$1\frac{2}{5}$	$3\frac{3}{7}$	$5\frac{3}{5}$	$7\frac{1}{3}$	$3\frac{1}{9}$

Lesson 6.4, page 68

1. $\frac{3}{7}$ 2. $1\frac{2}{5}$ 3. $4\frac{3}{5}$ 4. $1\frac{3}{4}$ 5. $\frac{1}{3}$ 6. $5\frac{2}{5}$

Lesson 6.5, page 69

	a	b	c	d	e
1.	$\frac{1}{4}$	$\frac{1}{2}$	$\frac{1}{2}$	$\frac{25}{56}$	$\frac{2}{9}$
2.	$\frac{13}{45}$	$\frac{11}{35}$	$\frac{7}{24}$	$\frac{1}{2}$	$\frac{19}{36}$
3.	$\frac{1}{5}$	$\frac{23}{26}$	$\frac{11}{24}$	$\frac{9}{20}$	$\frac{13}{35}$

Lesson 6.6, page 70

	a	b	c	d	e
1.	$2\frac{1}{2}$	$5\frac{1}{8}$	$2\frac{1}{2}$	$4\frac{3}{8}$	$1\frac{1}{9}$
2.	$2\frac{11}{56}$	$4\frac{1}{3}$	$5\frac{19}{40}$	$6\frac{2}{9}$	$3\frac{9}{70}$
3.	$5\frac{11}{12}$	$3\frac{7}{40}$	$3\frac{5}{12}$	$3\frac{9}{35}$	$2\frac{3}{4}$
4.	$1\frac{3}{22}$	$3\frac{13}{40}$	$1\frac{47}{72}$	$1\frac{1}{6}$	$7\frac{30}{77}$

Grade 5 Answers

Lesson 6.7, page 71

	a	b	c	d	e
1.	$\frac{4}{9}$	$\frac{3}{7}$	$\frac{3}{10}$	$\frac{1}{2}$	$\frac{1}{4}$
2.	$\frac{1}{4}$	$\frac{5}{36}$	$6\frac{7}{9}$	$\frac{2}{9}$	$2\frac{3}{7}$
3.	$8\frac{9}{10}$	$3\frac{1}{2}$	$5\frac{1}{4}$	$\frac{1}{8}$	5
4.	$6\frac{3}{11}$	$5\frac{4}{7}$	$1\frac{3}{5}$	$\frac{47}{72}$	$8\frac{1}{4}$
5.	$2\frac{2}{3}$	$2\frac{5}{24}$	$1\frac{5}{12}$	$2\frac{2}{33}$	$2\frac{1}{12}$

Lesson 6.8, page 72

1. $\frac{3}{14}$ 2. $\frac{17}{20}$ 3. $1\frac{1}{3}$ 4. $\frac{3}{8}$ 5. $\frac{19}{24}$ 6. $1\frac{7}{15}$

Posttest, page 73

	a	b	c	d
1.	$\frac{1}{3}$	$\frac{1}{7}$	$\frac{1}{4}$	$\frac{3}{8}$
2.	$\frac{1}{4}$	$3\frac{1}{6}$	$6\frac{1}{10}$	$1\frac{1}{2}$
3.	$2\frac{1}{3}$	$4\frac{4}{7}$	$2\frac{1}{3}$	$\frac{8}{21}$
4.	$\frac{55}{72}$	$\frac{28}{99}$	$\frac{11}{24}$	$2\frac{3}{8}$
5.	$3\frac{17}{18}$	$2\frac{4}{15}$	$1\frac{1}{28}$	$7\frac{14}{45}$

Posttest, page 74

6. $\frac{1}{2}$ 7. $\frac{1}{18}$ 8. $4\frac{1}{18}$ 9. $1\frac{1}{8}$ 10. $\frac{4}{5}$

Mid-Test

Mid-Test, page 75

	a	b	c	d
1.	128	121	163	340
2.	855	657	4042	7230
3.	80242	197142	1254430	1378
4.	5349	32890	18124	240102
5.	19	14	115	796
6.	288	535	1238	2787
7.	2389	8826	38814	56867
8.	89363	758856	185099	736687

Mid-Test, page 76

	a	b	c	d
9.	84	216	1248	30608
10.	9366	6768	29184	184383
11.	39283	209592	3310266	2846844
12.	4r2	3r3	53r3	52r4
13.	1608	431r6	33r4	70r14
14.	23r21	69r5	2108	443r7

Mid-Test, page 77

	a	b	c
15.	9	4	3
16.	3	19	9
17.	$2\frac{1}{4}$	$5\frac{2}{3}$	$11\frac{1}{3}$

18.	$4\frac{5}{12}$	$10\frac{1}{4}$	$9\frac{3}{7}$
19.	$\frac{13}{3}$	$\frac{68}{9}$	$\frac{17}{10}$
20.	$\frac{15}{4}$	$\frac{71}{12}$	$\frac{74}{9}$
21.	$\frac{9}{10}$	$\frac{4}{5}$	$2\frac{1}{6}$
22.	$3\frac{2}{3}$	$8\frac{1}{2}$	$7\frac{2}{3}$
23.	$6\frac{2}{5}$	$8\frac{1}{2}$	$11\frac{1}{4}$

Mid-Test, page 78

	a	b	c	d
24.	1	$\frac{31}{35}$	$1\frac{5}{24}$	$5\frac{2}{3}$
25.	$\frac{1}{2}$	0	$\frac{6}{55}$	$6\frac{1}{4}$
26.	7	$14\frac{2}{7}$	$17\frac{1}{21}$	$12\frac{3}{8}$
27.	$5\frac{5}{8}$	$4\frac{1}{6}$	$4\frac{1}{36}$	$1\frac{17}{24}$
28.	$12\frac{1}{10}$	$12\frac{20}{21}$	$2\frac{1}{2}$	$4\frac{5}{6}$

Chapter 7

Pretest, page 79

	a	b	c
1.	$\frac{1}{6}$	$\frac{3}{14}$	$\frac{1}{5}$
2.	$\frac{1}{4}$	$\frac{2}{9}$	$1\frac{3}{7}$
3.	$2\frac{2}{5}$	6	$1\frac{1}{2}$
4.	$11\frac{3}{7}$	22	$6\frac{3}{7}$
5.	$17\frac{1}{2}$	$18\frac{1}{2}$	$3\frac{17}{20}$
6.	7	$5\frac{8}{9}$	$14\frac{3}{10}$

Pretest, page 80

7. $\frac{8}{15}$ 8. $2\frac{1}{4}$ 9. $5\frac{1}{7}$ 10. $227\frac{1}{4}$ 11. $6\frac{6}{7}$ 12. $12\frac{4}{9}$

Lesson 7.1, page 81

	a	b	c
1.	$\frac{2}{27}$	$\frac{1}{20}$	$\frac{9}{28}$
2.	$\frac{5}{16}$	$\frac{5}{21}$	$\frac{1}{11}$
3.	$\frac{2}{5}$	$\frac{1}{7}$	$\frac{4}{27}$
4.	$\frac{14}{25}$	$\frac{1}{4}$	$\frac{5}{22}$
5.	$\frac{5}{9}$	$\frac{27}{40}$	$\frac{49}{132}$

Lesson 7.2, page 82

	a	b	c	d
1.	$\frac{3}{8}$	$3\frac{1}{3}$	$1\frac{7}{9}$	$1\frac{1}{7}$
2.	$3\frac{3}{5}$	$1\frac{1}{9}$	$\frac{6}{7}$	$5\frac{1}{4}$
3.	$3\frac{5}{9}$	4	$4\frac{4}{5}$	3
4.	$1\frac{1}{2}$	2	$7\frac{7}{8}$	$3\frac{9}{11}$
5.	$3\frac{1}{9}$	$2\frac{7}{10}$	$1\frac{1}{6}$	$5\frac{5}{7}$

Grade 5 Answers

Lesson 7.3, page 83

	a	b	c	d
1.	$4\frac{4}{5}$	$18\frac{1}{3}$	$25\frac{5}{7}$	$7\frac{1}{5}$
2.	$36\frac{1}{6}$	$8\frac{1}{2}$	$19\frac{1}{3}$	$33\frac{1}{7}$
3.	$5\frac{1}{5}$	$14\frac{1}{4}$	$15\frac{5}{8}$	$14\frac{1}{2}$
4.	$26\frac{2}{5}$	10	$4\frac{2}{3}$	$5\frac{3}{4}$
5.	$20\frac{2}{5}$	$37\frac{1}{7}$	$59\frac{8}{9}$	$7\frac{3}{7}$

Lesson 7.4, page 84

	a	b	c	d
1.	$7\frac{1}{2}$	$6\frac{5}{12}$	$15\frac{1}{6}$	$4\frac{20}{21}$
2.	$8\frac{3}{40}$	$14\frac{32}{35}$	$5\frac{4}{9}$	$14\frac{4}{27}$
3.	$12\frac{3}{5}$	$8\frac{13}{15}$	$21\frac{5}{7}$	$14\frac{34}{49}$
4.	$20\frac{5}{12}$	$5\frac{5}{64}$	9	$12\frac{4}{15}$
5.	$4\frac{35}{72}$	$16\frac{1}{4}$	$6\frac{29}{32}$	39

Lesson 7.5, page 85

	a	b	c	d
1.	$\frac{3}{10}$	$\frac{8}{21}$	$\frac{2}{3}$	$\frac{1}{8}$
2.	$\frac{2}{9}$	$1\frac{1}{7}$	$2\frac{2}{3}$	$\frac{3}{5}$
3.	$2\frac{2}{3}$	2	$1\frac{1}{2}$	5
4.	$19\frac{1}{4}$	$\frac{3}{4}$	$4\frac{9}{14}$	$12\frac{1}{4}$
5.	$16\frac{13}{18}$	$17\frac{1}{5}$	$10\frac{1}{2}$	$15\frac{1}{2}$
6.	$7\frac{7}{16}$	$14\frac{2}{3}$	$6\frac{3}{5}$	$10\frac{20}{21}$

Lesson 7.6, page 86

1. $\frac{8}{15}$ 2. $\frac{1}{12}$ 3. $1\frac{1}{3}$ 4. $2\frac{1}{12}$ 5. $\frac{3}{7}$ 6. 14

Posttest, page 87

	a	b	c
1.	$\frac{2}{9}$	$\frac{1}{2}$	$\frac{5}{14}$
2.	$\frac{11}{18}$	$\frac{12}{35}$	$\frac{9}{32}$
3.	$1\frac{7}{8}$	$\frac{2}{3}$	3
4.	$3\frac{8}{9}$	10	$37\frac{1}{2}$
5.	$7\frac{1}{6}$	$14\frac{4}{7}$	$7\frac{19}{24}$
6.	$12\frac{3}{8}$	$11\frac{7}{8}$	$26\frac{5}{21}$

Posttest, page 88

7. $\frac{1}{4}$ 8. $5\frac{1}{7}$ 9. $13\frac{1}{5}$ 10. $4\frac{1}{5}$ 11. $1\frac{5}{18}$ 12. $73\frac{1}{3}$

Chapter 8

Pretest, page 89

	a	b	c	d
1.	$6\frac{2}{3}$	$\frac{1}{16}$	$\frac{1}{9}$	$1\frac{1}{3}$
2.	$\frac{1}{15}$	$\frac{1}{8}$	$\frac{14}{15}$	$\frac{1}{2}$
3.	$3\frac{1}{2}$	$1\frac{3}{25}$	$2\frac{4}{9}$	$\frac{8}{45}$
4.	$\frac{4}{15}$	$\frac{3}{8}$	$3\frac{2}{3}$	$\frac{4}{7}$
5.	$1\frac{1}{4}$	$1\frac{4}{5}$	$\frac{5}{11}$	$\frac{624}{707}$

Pretest, page 90

6. $\frac{11}{18}$ 7. 3 8. $1\frac{17}{32}$ 9. $1\frac{7}{10}$ 10. $4\frac{1}{12}$

Lesson 8.1, page 91

	a	b	c	d	e	f
1.	$\frac{5}{4}$	3	$\frac{8}{7}$	$\frac{10}{9}$	$\frac{5}{3}$	$\frac{7}{4}$
2.	$\frac{4}{3}$	$\frac{8}{5}$	$\frac{12}{5}$	$\frac{3}{5}$	8	$\frac{3}{2}$
3.	$\frac{1}{9}$	$\frac{7}{10}$	5	$\frac{2}{9}$	$\frac{2}{3}$	$\frac{1}{6}$
4.	$\frac{9}{7}$	$\frac{1}{8}$	$\frac{7}{12}$	$\frac{1}{2}$	9	$\frac{12}{11}$
5.	11	$\frac{5}{9}$	$\frac{1}{5}$	$\frac{5}{8}$	$\frac{1}{9}$	$\frac{7}{5}$
6.	$\frac{12}{7}$	$\frac{1}{15}$	$\frac{2}{5}$	$\frac{1}{7}$	$\frac{7}{11}$	$\frac{17}{3}$
7.	14	$\frac{1}{11}$	$\frac{1}{13}$	$\frac{4}{15}$	$\frac{16}{5}$	$\frac{1}{12}$
8.	$\frac{1}{4}$	$\frac{4}{5}$	$\frac{4}{11}$	12	$\frac{6}{7}$	$\frac{10}{11}$
9.	$\frac{1}{3}$	$\frac{19}{4}$	$\frac{1}{16}$	$\frac{11}{8}$	$\frac{1}{5}$	$\frac{11}{18}$

Lesson 8.2, page 92

	a	b	c	d
1.	$\frac{2}{9}$	$6\frac{2}{3}$	$\frac{1}{10}$	$\frac{1}{6}$
2.	$\frac{5}{24}$	15	10	$\frac{1}{18}$
3.	11	$\frac{2}{7}$	$6\frac{6}{7}$	$\frac{1}{18}$
4.	27	$\frac{5}{54}$	7	$\frac{1}{16}$

Lesson 8.3, page 93

	a	b	c	d
1.	$\frac{2}{3}$	8	$\frac{2}{3}$	$1\frac{1}{2}$
2.	$\frac{5}{6}$	$\frac{2}{3}$	$\frac{7}{10}$	$2\frac{1}{4}$
3.	$4\frac{2}{7}$	$\frac{3}{4}$	2	$\frac{2}{3}$
4.	$2\frac{1}{3}$	$\frac{11}{24}$	$1\frac{1}{48}$	$\frac{25}{28}$

Lesson 8.4, page 94

	a	b	c	d
1.	$\frac{7}{8}$	$\frac{1}{3}$	$\frac{2}{3}$	$\frac{2}{11}$
2.	$\frac{2}{5}$	3	$1\frac{1}{2}$	$1\frac{1}{5}$
3.	$1\frac{3}{4}$	$\frac{5}{7}$	$\frac{35}{54}$	$\frac{10}{21}$

Lesson 8.5, page 95

	a	b	c	d
1.	$\frac{1}{14}$	$\frac{1}{36}$	$\frac{1}{12}$	$5\frac{1}{2}$
2.	$3\frac{3}{4}$	$\frac{5}{12}$	$\frac{11}{72}$	$\frac{1}{8}$
3.	$\frac{5}{6}$	$\frac{3}{4}$	$\frac{3}{8}$	2
4.	$1\frac{2}{3}$	$\frac{5}{12}$	$\frac{36}{55}$	$1\frac{1}{98}$
5.	$8\frac{26}{27}$	$1\frac{9}{11}$	$\frac{10}{27}$	$\frac{1}{2}$

Lesson 8.6, page 96

1. $5\frac{1}{4}$ 2. $\frac{1}{14}$ 3. $14\frac{2}{5}$ 4. $\frac{3}{8}$ 5. $4\frac{5}{32}$ 6. 2

Grade 5 Answers

Posttest, page 97

	a	b	c	d
1.	48	$6\frac{2}{3}$	$\frac{2}{9}$	$\frac{1}{15}$
2.	$\frac{2}{3}$	$\frac{1}{10}$	1	$\frac{25}{27}$
3.	3	$\frac{3}{4}$	$2\frac{2}{3}$	$\frac{3}{10}$
4.	$\frac{1}{5}$	$\frac{3}{28}$	$1\frac{1}{2}$	$\frac{5}{16}$
5.	$1\frac{9}{19}$	$\frac{46}{79}$	$\frac{7}{9}$	$\frac{28}{171}$

Posttest, page 98

6. $\frac{1}{4}$ 7. $1\frac{1}{7}$

8. 3   9. $4\frac{1}{5}$

10. $10\frac{1}{2}$ 11. $\frac{7}{20}$

Chapter 9

Pretest, page 99

	a	b
1.	2 yd.	15840 ft.
2.	7 ft.	144 in.
3.	105 in.	13960 ft.
4.	8 pt.	26 c.
5.	20 qt.	12 c.
6.	15 qt.	13 pt.
7.	48 oz.	9 lb.
8.	8 T.	5,550 lb.
9.	133 oz.	194 oz.
10.	20 ft.	16 in.
11.	21 ft.	18 yd.

Pretest, page 100

	a	b
12.	9 sq. ft.	16 sq. yd.
13.	36 cubic in.	64 cubic ft.
14.	2,100 sq. ft.	
15.	1,200 cubic in.	

Lesson 9.1, page 101

	a	b	c
1.	4 yd.	10 ft.	9 ft.
2.	18 ft.	10,560 ft.	9 yd.
3.	12 yd.	120 in.	1,760 yd.
4.	57 in.	27 ft.	11,282 ft.
5.	36 in.	14 ft.	9 yd.
6.	98 in.	6 yd.	72 in.
7.	144 in.	60 in.	8 ft.
8.	5,627 ft.	7,040 yd.	5 ft.
9.	252 in.	3 yd.	134 in.
10.	116 in.	5,286 ft.	2 yd.
11.	13,801 ft.	10 ft.	1,764 yd.
12.	7 yd.	16 ft.	182 in.

Lesson 9.2, page 102

	a	b	c
1.	3 pt.	2 qt.	8 c.
2.	5 qt.	18 c.	6 pt.
3.	8 qt.	12 c.	6 c.
4.	28 c.	16 pt.	16 c.
5.	7 pt.	16 qt.	9 qt.
6.	16 c.	5 c.	48 c.
7.	43 c.	23 c.	27 c.
8.	64 pt.	3 gal.	6 pt.
9.	19 qt.	14 c.	17 pt.
10.	20 c.	11 c.	11 qt.
11.	30 c.	12 pt.	30 c.
12.	27 pt.	22 c.	36 c.

Lesson 9.3, page 103

	a	b	c
1.	32 oz.	2 lb.	8,000 lb.
2.	14,000 lb.	112 oz.	3 lb.
3.	5 lb.	32,000 oz.	4,000 lb.
4.	80 oz.	2,350 lb.	20,000 lb.
5.	7 T.	128 oz.	21 oz.
6.	51 oz.	10 lb.	4,792 lb.
7.	32,005 oz.	9 lb.	14 T.
8.	4 T.	55 oz.	160,000 oz.
9.	40 oz.	7,240 lb.	15 T.
10.	197 oz.	21,344 lb.	96,822 oz.

Lesson 9.4, page 104

1. 32°   2. 98.6°   3. 212°

Lesson 9.5, page 105

	a	b
1.	2 hr. 38 min.	10 hr. 33 min.
2.	7 hr. 5 min.	6 hr. 24 min.
3a.	12:15 a.m.; 2:51 a.m.; 2 hr. 36 min.	
3b.	3:37 p.m.; 10:35 p.m.; 6 hr. 58 min.	

Lesson 9.6, page 106

1. 25 c.
2. 64 oz.; 4 lb.
3. 27 qt.
4. 2,550 ft.; 405 ft.; 715 yd.; 135 yd.
5. 28,800 oz.; 9,800 oz.
6. 8 hr. 32 min.

Lesson 9.7, page 107

	a	b	c
1.	20 in.	19 yd.	32 ft.
2.	20 ft.	48 in.	24 in.
3.	19 yd.	18 yd.	12 yd.
4.	22 ft.	25 in.	40 ft.

Grade 5 Answers

Lesson 9.8, page 108

	a	b	c
1.	15 sq. in.	16 sq. ft.	16 sq. ft.
2.	14 sq. yd.	49 sq. in.	6 sq. yd.
3.	64 sq. ft.	45 sq. in.	30 sq. yd.

Lesson 9.9, page 109

	a	b	c
1.	8 cubic in.	48 cubic yd.	15 cubic ft.
2.	36 cubic yd.	126 cubic ft.	90 cubic ft.
3.	112 cubic in.	60 cubic yd.	189 cubic ft.
4.	56 cubic yd.	144 cubic ft.	140 cubic in.

Lesson 9.10, page 110

1. 122 ft. 2. 24 sq. in. 3. 76 ft.
4. 1,188 cubic yd. 5. 8 ft. 6. 600 cubic in.

Posttest, page 111

	a	b
1.	27 ft.	3 yd.
2.	19 ft.	93 in.
3.	21,320 ft.	4,020 yd.
4.	34 c.	24 qt.
5.	36 pt.	37 pt.
6.	34 qt.	31 c.
7.	192 oz.	7 lb.
8.	28,000 lb.	75 oz.
9.	170 oz.	3,856 lb.
10.	8 hr. 17 min.	14 hr. 13 min.
11.	26 ft.	13 in.

Posttest, page 112

	a	b
12.	12 sq. in.	72 sq. ft.
13.	18 cubic ft.	160 cubic in.
14.	8 hr. 55 min.	15. 35 sq. yd.

Chapter 10

Pretest, page 113

1a. 50 cm 1b. 8,000 m 1c. 5,000,000 mm
2a. 3 m 2b. 3 km 2c. 3,200 m
3a. 6,000 mL 3b. 15,000 L 3c. 4,000,000 mL
4a. 2 kL 4b. 7 kL 4c. 12 L
5a. 8,000 g 5b. 5,000 mg 5c. 7 g
6a. 17 kg 6b. 36 kg 6c. 3,500 g
7a. 22 cm 7b. 11 km 7c. 25 m

Pretest, page 114

	a	b	c
8.	16 sq. mm	1 sq. m	32 sq. m
9.	10 sq. m	81 sq. cm	24 sq. cm
10.	64 cubic m	84 cubic m	512 cubic m
11.	200 sq. m		

Lesson 10.1, page 115

	a	b	c
1.	500 cm	2 cm	200,000 cm
2.	7,000 m	3 km	2 m
3.	60 cm	8,000 mm	9 m
4.	5 m	450 mm	2,700 cm
5.	42,000	12,000 m	80,000
6.	Answers will vary.	7. Duane's; 6 mm	8. 28 m

Lesson 10.2, page 116

	a	b	c
1.	3,000 L	6,000 mL	8 L
2.	4 kL	51 L	5 kL
3.	18,000 mL	2,000,000 mL	22,000 L
4.	4,000,000 mL	46 kL	11,000 mL
5.	32 L	2,200 mL	12 kL
6.	4,000 mL	3,600 L	2,005,000 mL
7.	5,000 L	16 kL	8,772 mL
8.	4,000 mL	9. 7,000 mL; Marcus; 1,400 mL	

Lesson 10.3, page 117

	a	b	c
1.	5,000 mg	17 kg	2,000,000 mg
2.	4,000 g	2 g	8,433,000 mg
3.	7,000,000 mg	14,000 mg	18,000 g
4.	8 g	25,000 g	11 kg
5.	23,000 mg	19 kg	32 g
6.	2,150 mg	4,200 g	5,273 mg
7.	2,821 g	3,000 g	14,360 mg
8.	256,000 mg	22,840 mg	9,000 mg
9.	Pedro's; 20,700 mg		

Lesson 10.4, page 118

1. Ramon; 9,000 g 2. 82,000 m 3. 90 mm
4. 236,000,000 mL; 236 kL
5. 2,292,000 mg 6. 16,000 mL

Lesson 10.5, page 119

1. 0°C 2. 100°C 3. 37°C

Lesson 10.6, page 120

	a	b	c
1.	16 m	10 mm	20 cm
2.	18 km	26 m	21 m
3.	82 mm	50 m	96 km

Lesson 10.7, page 121

	a	b	c
1.	8 cubic m	60 cubic m	36 cubic m
2.	42 cubic cm	144 cubic cm	54 cubic m
3.	24 cubic m	100 cubic m	216 cubic m

Lesson 10.8, page 122

1. 270 m 2. 9 cm 3. 14 km 4. 135 sq. m
5. 24 sq. m 6. 144 cubic m

Grade 5 Answers

Posttest, page 123

	a	b
1.	16,000 m	636 cm
2.	88 mm	4,850 mm
3.	7,000 L	10 L
4.	13,000,000 mL	15,700 mL
5.	22,000 g	8,942 mg
6.	14 mm	26 km
7.	20 m	19 m

Posttest, page 124

	a	b	c
8.	4 sq. m	15 sq. cm	48 sq. cm
9.	12 cubic cm	45 cubic cm	8 cubic m
10.	147 cubic mm	100 cubic m	450 cubic cm
11.	30 cubic m		

Chapter 11

Pretest, page 125
1. 25 2. blue 3. yellow 4. 20 5. 105
6. 4 7. 15 8. 16 9. 46

Pretest, page 126
10. 17 11. 280 12. 50 yd. 13. 3282
14. 20; 20; 15 15. 94; 91; 15
16. 821; 815; 18 17. $\frac{1}{4}$; $\frac{1}{3}$; $\frac{5}{12}$ 18. $\frac{1}{4}$; $\frac{3}{8}$; $\frac{1}{4}$; $\frac{1}{8}$

Lesson 11.1, page 127
1. crackers, apples, oranges, sandwiches, celery
2. 25 3. 20 4. 60 5. 25
6. crackers and sandwiches 7. 125

Lesson 11.1, page 128

Favorite Musical Instruments

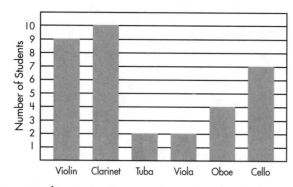

1. favorite instruments 2. number of students
3. clarinet 4. tuba; viola 5. 8 6. 34

Lesson 11.2, page 129
1. 155 2. 30 3. Aug. and Sept. 4. May
5. October 6. 65

Lesson 11.2, page 130

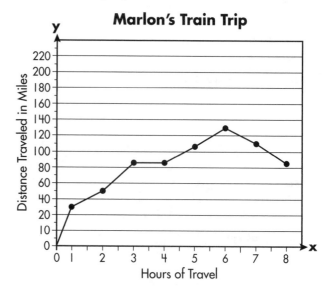

1. hours of travel 2. distance traveled each hour
3. hour 6 4. hour 1 5. hour 6 6. 682 mi.

Lesson 11.3, page 131
1. 5 2. 27 3. 14 4. 16 5. 37 6. 11 yd.
7. 29 in. 8. 55 m 9. 40 10. 86

Lesson 11.3, page 132
1. $66 2. 20 points 3. 9 hours
4. 9 hours 5. 6 hours

Lesson 11.4, page 133
1. 7; 9; 7 2. 6; 4; 5 3. 11; 11; 14
4. 24; 24; 17 5. $27; $38; $17
6. 5 mi.; 2 mi.; 7 mi. 7. 163; 163; 18
8. $71; $71; $15

Lesson 11.4, page 134
1. 58 in.; 58 in.; 10 in. 2. 18; 22; 13
3. $16; $12; $10 4. $105; $108; $12

Lesson 11.5, page 135
1a. $\frac{3}{14}$ 1b. $\frac{1}{7}$ 1c. $\frac{2}{7}$ 1d. $\frac{1}{14}$ 1e. $\frac{1}{7}$
1f. $\frac{1}{14}$ 1g. $\frac{1}{14}$ 1h. 1
2. $\frac{1}{2}$; $\frac{1}{2}$ 3. $\frac{1}{2}$; $\frac{1}{2}$

Lesson 11.5, page 136
1. $\frac{1}{10}$ 2. $\frac{2}{25}$; $\frac{4}{5}$; $\frac{3}{25}$ 3. $\frac{1}{3}$; $\frac{1}{6}$; $\frac{1}{2}$ 4. $\frac{5}{12}$; $\frac{1}{3}$; $\frac{1}{4}$

Posttest, page 137
1. hours of sleep 2. number of students 3. 45
4. 25 5. 115 6. 30 lb. 7. 70 lb.
8. 4 years 9. 2–3 10. 0–1

Grade 5 Answers

Posttest, page 138
11. 7   **12.** 64   **13.** 21   **14.** 12 in.   **15.** $44
16. 1401   **17.** 12; 9; 9   **18.** 19; 19; 12
19. 71; 68; 8   **20.** $180; $177; $13   **21.** $\frac{1}{3}$; $\frac{1}{8}$; $\frac{13}{24}$

Chapter 12

Pretest, page 139

	a	b
1.	line segment; $\overline{AB}$	line; $\overleftrightarrow{XY}$
2.	ray; $\overrightarrow{PQ}$	line; $\overleftrightarrow{GH}$
3.	intersecting	parallel
4.	intersecting	perpendicular
5.	acute; $\angle XYZ$	obtuse; $\angle PQR$
6.	obtuse; $\angle ABC$	acute; $\angle 123$

Pretest, page 140
7a. 30°   **7b.** 135°
8. 1   **9.** 4   **10.** 3   **11.** 2

	a	b
12.	quadrilateral; rectangle	triangle
13.	quadrilateral; square	hexagon
14.	flat	curved; flat

Lesson 12.1, page 141

	a	b
1.	line segment, $\overline{PQ}$	line, $\overleftrightarrow{AB}$
2.	ray, $\overrightarrow{RS}$	point, R
3.	line, $\overleftrightarrow{GH}$	ray, $\overrightarrow{PQ}$

Lesson 12.1, page 142

	a	b
1.	Rays: $\overrightarrow{QP}$; $\overrightarrow{QR}$ Vertex: Q Angle: $\angle PQR$	Rays: $\overrightarrow{ED}$; $\overrightarrow{EF}$ Vertex: E Angle: $\angle DEF$
2.	Rays: $\overrightarrow{ML}$; $\overrightarrow{MN}$ Vertex: M Angle: $\angle LMN$	Rays: $\overrightarrow{BA}$; $\overrightarrow{BC}$ Vertex: B Angle: $\angle ABC$
3.	Rays: $\overrightarrow{21}$; $\overrightarrow{23}$ Vertex: 2 Angle: $\angle 123$	Rays: $\overrightarrow{SR}$; $\overrightarrow{ST}$ Vertex: S Angle: $\angle RST$
4.	Rays: $\overrightarrow{YX}$; $\overrightarrow{YZ}$ Vertex: Y Angle: $\angle XYZ$	Rays: $\overrightarrow{76}$; $\overrightarrow{78}$ Vertex: 7 Angle: $\angle 678$

Lesson 12.2, page 143

	a	b
1.	intersecting	parallel
2.	parallel	perpendicular
3.	perpendicular	intersecting
4.	intersecting	parallel

Lesson 12.3, page 144

	a	b
1.	acute	acute
2.	obtuse	acute
3.	right	obtuse

Lesson 12.3, page 145

	a	b
1.	$\angle ABC = 60°$	$\angle GHI = 90°$
2.	$\angle PQR = 110°$	$\angle XYZ = 170°$
3.	$\angle 123 = 90°$	$\angle ABC = 30°$
4.	$\angle ABC = 60°$; acute $\angle BAC = 60°$; acute $\angle BCA = 60°$; acute	$\angle XYZ = 90°$; right $\angle YZX = 45°$; acute $\angle XZY = 45°$; acute

Lesson 12.4, page 146

	a	b	c
1.	rectangle	trapezoid	rhombus
2.	trapezoid	parallelogram	kite

Lesson 12.5, page 147

	a	b	c
1.	pentagon	quadrilateral	triangle
2.	pentagon	triangle	hexagon
3.	octagon	quadrilateral	heptagon

Lesson 12.6, page 148
1. cube; 6; 12; 8; flat
2. square pyramid; 8; 4; 1; 5; 5
3. cylinder; 2; flat, curved

Posttest, page 149

	a	b
1.	line; $\overleftrightarrow{PQ}$	ray; $\overrightarrow{YZ}$
2.	line segment; $\overline{AB}$	ray; $\overrightarrow{RS}$
3.	parallel	intersecting
4.	perpendicular	intersecting
5.	acute; $\angle PQR$	acute; $\angle ABC$
6.	right; $\angle VWX$	obtuse; $\angle XYZ$

Posttest, page 150

	a	b
7.	87°	156°
8.	square	trapezoid
9.	kite	rhombus

10. 2   **11.** 1   **12.** 3

	a	b
13.	faces: 5 edges: 8 vertices: 5 type: square pyramid	faces: 6 edges: 12 vertices: 8 type: rectangular prism

Grade 5 Answers

Chapter 13

Pretest, page 151

	a	b
1.	16, 18, 20	50, 57, 64
2.	85, 82, 79	25, 15, 5
3.	16, 22, 29	80, 110, 145
4.	30, 18, 4	20, 24, 28
5.	64, 128, 256	27, 9, 3

6a. number of leaves in a pile **6b.** the height of a tree
7a. x **7b.** number of videos in a store

Pretest, page 152

	a	b
8.	$x + 50$	$x + 15$
9.	$40 \div p$	$20 \times a$
10.	$x - 13$	$22 \times t$

11a. t plus 33 equals 72. **11b.** 14 plus x equals 30.
12a. y minus 4 equals 23.
12b. 6 multiplied by y equals 12.
13. 140; $120 + y = 260$ **14.** 4; $9 \times y = 36$

Lesson 13.1, page 153

	a	b
1.	19, 22, 25	30, 35, 40
2.	6, 5, 4	30, 24, 18
3.	27, 33, 40	148, 150, 152
4.	63, 102, 165	72, 63, 54
5.	44, 58, 74	21, 24, 27

Lesson 13.2, page 154

1a. number of weeks; $x + 2$
1b. number of extra cherries; $3 + x$
2a. x; $x + 8$
2b. amount of corn in field; $x + 10$
3a. y; $y - 32$ **3b.** cookies in a bag; $5 + x$
4a. length of fence; $8 + x$ **4b.** p; $61 + p$
5a. number of plants; $4 \times y$ **5b.** y; $6 \times y$
6a. p; $p \div 9$ **6b.** number of decks; $5 \times d$

Lesson 13.3, page 155

1a. x plus 3 equals 7. **1b.** x plus 9 equals 12.
2a. 25 plus r equals 41. **2b.** r minus 11 equals 28.
3a. 58 minus x equals 17. **3b.** 10 times k equals 90.
4a. 18 minus y equals 10. **4b.** 4 times t equals 64.
5a. 12 divided by x equals 3.
5b. 100 divided by p equals 25.
6a. $8 \div 2 = y$ **6b.** $12 + y = 14$
7a. $y \times 7 = 14$ **7b.** $y - 14 = 6$

Lesson 13.4, page 156

1. 3493 **2.** 250; 200 **3.** 7; 10; 13
4. $19 + y = 30$

Posttest, page 157

1a. 46, 55, 64 **1b.** 36, 24, 12
2a. 6271, 6303, 6367 **2b.** 24, 28, 32
3a. 30, 38, 47 **3b.** 64, 32, 16
4a. number of lightbulbs in a house **4b.** y
5a. amount of clothes in a load **5b.** number of eggs
6a. $x + 13$ **6b.** $x + 32$ **7a.** $x - 55$ **7b.** $3 \times a$
8a. $b \times 6$ **8b.** $x \div 3$

Posttest, page 158

9a. 7 plus x equals 21. **9b.** 50 minus y equals 35.
10a. s multiplied by 12 equals 84.
10b. x minus 20 equals 13.
11a. 14 divided by y equals 2.
11b. 36 divided by r equals 4.
12a. 17 plus x equals 35. **12b.** 38 minus t equals 16.
13. 32; 64 **14.** $49 \div y = 7$ **15.** $32 - y = 24$

Final Test

Final Test, page 159

	a	b	c	d
1.	125	843	5716	96302
2.	25	263	3875	35528
3.	734406	2073	84713	497606
4.	126	544	894	15714
5.	36r1	1091	134r2	1398r18
6.	492246	451860	2003184	1847200

Final Test, page 160

	a	b	c	d
7.	$\frac{41}{60}$	$1\frac{1}{5}$	$9\frac{3}{5}$	$6\frac{5}{14}$
8.	$\frac{1}{2}$	$1\frac{13}{18}$	$5\frac{3}{7}$	$3\frac{11}{12}$
9.	$\frac{2}{7}$	$\frac{3}{8}$	$\frac{7}{32}$	$\frac{9}{11}$
10.	$2\frac{1}{4}$	$\frac{2}{3}$	$1\frac{5}{9}$	$\frac{3}{4}$
11.	$6\frac{2}{3}$	$16\frac{9}{10}$	$12\frac{3}{5}$	8

Final Test, page 161

	a	b	c
12.	2 cm	3000 cm	21000 m
13.	17000 L	18 L	2972 L
14.	17 m	22 yd.	15 ft.
15.	8 sq. ft.	30 sq. in.	25 sq. cm
16.	56 cubic yd.	125 cubic ft.	72 cubic in.

Final Test, page 162

17. 5 **18.** 8 **19.** 7 **20.** 6 **21.** 3 **22.** 4
23. 9 **24.** 2 **25.** 1 **26.** 10

27.	$4\frac{1}{3}$	19	$70
	4	17	$71
	2	12	$65
	5	17	$10
28.	triangle	hexagon	quadrilateral

Notes

Notes

Notes

Notes